LAW SCHOOL EXAMS

Preparing and Writing to Win

Editorial Advisors

LAW SCHOOL EXAMS

Preparing and Writing to Win

Second Edition

Charles R. Calleros

Professor of Law
Arizona State University

Wolters Kluwer
Law & Business

Published by Wolters Kluwer Law & Business in New York.

Wolters Kluwer Law & Business serves customers worldwide with CCH, Aspen Publishers, and Kluwer Law International products. (www.wolterskluwerlb.com)

To contact Customer Service, e-mail customer.service@wolterskluwer.com, call 1-800-234-1660, fax 1-800-901-9075, or mail correspondence to:

Wolters Kluwer Law & Business
Attn: Order Department
PO Box 990
Frederick, MD 21705

Printed in the United States of America.

1 2 3 4 5 6 7 8 9 0

ISBN 978-1-4548-2701-6

Library of Congress Cataloging-in-Publication Data

Calleros, Charles R.
Law school exams : preparing and writing to win / Charles Calleros, professor of law, Arizona State University. – Second edition.
    pages cm
Includes bibliographical references.
ISBN 978-1-4548-2701-6
1. Law examinations — United States — Study guides. 2. Law — Study and teaching — United States. I. Title.
KF283.C35 2013
340.071′173–dc23

2013006405

About Wolters Kluwer Law & Business

Wolters Kluwer Law & Business is a leading global provider of intelligent information and digital solutions for legal and business professionals in key specialty areas, and respected educational resources for professors and law students. Wolters Kluwer Law & Business connects legal and business professionals as well as those in the education market with timely, specialized authoritative content and information-enabled solutions to support success through productivity, accuracy and mobility.

Serving customers worldwide, Wolters Kluwer Law & Business products include those under the Aspen Publishers, CCH, Kluwer Law International, Loislaw, Best Case, ftwilliam.com and MediRegs family of products.

CCH products have been a trusted resource since 1913, and are highly regarded resources for legal, securities, antitrust and trade regulation, government contracting, banking, pension, payroll, employment and labor, and healthcare reimbursement and compliance professionals.

Aspen Publishers products provide essential information to attorneys, business professionals and law students. Written by preeminent authorities, the product line offers analytical and practical information in a range of specialty practice areas from securities law and intellectual property to mergers and acquisitions and pension/benefits. Aspen's trusted legal education resources provide professors and students with high-quality, up-to-date and effective resources for successful instruction and study in all areas of the law.

Kluwer Law International products provide the global business community with reliable international legal information in English. Legal practitioners, corporate counsel and business executives around the world rely on Kluwer Law journals, looseleafs, books, and electronic products for comprehensive information in many areas of international legal practice.

Loislaw is a comprehensive online legal research product providing legal content to law firm practitioners of various specializations. Loislaw provides attorneys with the ability to quickly and efficiently find the necessary legal information they need, when and where they need it, by facilitating access to primary law as well as state-specific law, records, forms and treatises.

Best Case Solutions is the leading bankruptcy software product to the bankruptcy industry. It provides software and workflow tools to flawlessly streamline petition preparation and the electronic filing process, while timely incorporating ever-changing court requirements.

ftwilliam.com offers employee benefits professionals the highest quality plan documents (retirement, welfare and non-qualified) and government forms (5500/PBGC, 1099 and IRS) software at highly competitive prices.

MediRegs products provide integrated health care compliance content and software solutions for professionals in healthcare, higher education and life sciences, including professionals in accounting, law and consulting.

Wolters Kluwer Law & Business, a division of Wolters Kluwer, is headquartered in New York. Wolters Kluwer is a market-leading global information services company focused on professionals.

To my wonderful mother, Emily,
sharp and strong at 91.

Countless dedicated and hard-working law school graduates enjoy successful and satisfying careers in the law even though they did not excel on law school examinations. Good grades in law school, however, undeniably will open doors for you and greatly increase your options.

Indeed, grades earned in the first year and even in the first semester can have a disproportionate effect on the range of opportunities open to you. Good grades in the first year can open doors to a summer clerkship or a position on a law journal, which in turn can pave the way to other opportunities.

Notably, your grade in a typical law course is based entirely — or nearly entirely — on your performance on a single examination at the end of the semester. Consequently, it is imperative that you understand the nature of law school examinations, learn how to prepare well for them, and do your best on them by applying sound examination technique.

Unfortunately, most law schools provide the general student body with little or no instruction on the examination process. This creates the possibility that you can learn the law thoroughly and yet fail to perform your best on the all-important examination. This book seeks to close that gap by empowering you to apply your accumulated skills and knowledge to exams in the most effective possible manner.

For the first edition, the author thanks Alison Ewing, then Head Access Services and Reference Librarian at the Arizona State University Ross-Blakely Law Library, for her research assistance, and he thanks Nora Nuñez and Agnes Felton, then students at the law school, for their extremely helpful editing suggestions.

For the second edition, the author thanks his colleague, Professor Bob Dauber, for contributing the civil procedure multiple-choice questions employed as an exercise near the end of Chapter 12.

ACKNOWLEDGMENTS

Many thanks to 1L Alyssa Whetstine for her excellent proofreading and editing of the proof pages of the second edition and to Julie Nahil of Wolters Kluwer for her first-rate editing of the manuscript for the second edition.

PART ONE

OVERVIEW

Congratulations! You presumably are reading this book because you have been accepted to law school, thus demonstrating that you are among the best, brightest, and most highly motivated students in our society.

You likely will find the study of law to be both extremely challenging and remarkably different in nature from your undergraduate courses of study. Because your grade in a typical course will be based entirely on your performance on a single final exam, you should study the art of preparing for and taking law school exams in addition to studying the law itself.

The best way to use this book is to read it from cover to cover as early as possible, either before you commence your study of law or near the beginning of your first semester, because it might influence the study techniques that you adopt. You will soon appreciate that success on law school exams requires a sustained effort throughout the semester, starting with careful planning, followed by diligent study, and culminating in application of sound exam techniques. If you finish this book before or shortly after commencing your studies, you should have a much clearer vision of your first-semester goals and the means of achieving them.

The first two chapters of this book provide you with an orientation of sorts, by summarizing the steps to success in law school and by identifying the various types of law school exams that you might encounter. Having thus glimpsed your destination and the stops along the way, you will be better prepared to begin your exploration of the best means of preparing for law school exams, beginning in Chapter 3.

CHAPTER 1

Overview: A Recipe for Success in Law School

To help you devise a strategy for studying law and earning good grades, the chapters of this book address a broad range of topics, from the nature of legal analysis to techniques for succeeding on examinations. The following overview of topics provides you with a general roadmap for your journey through this book.

I. ATTITUDE: A MINDSET FOR SUCCESS

At various places, this book discusses the importance of maintaining a positive and constructive attitude. You can't bluff your way to good grades in law school, but you can do your best if you approach exams with the confidence that comes with thorough preparation.

A. Motivated for Success While Maintaining Collegiality

You should enter law school with enthusiasm and an understanding of the challenges awaiting you. You need not be overly competitive with your classmates; instead, collaborate with them in a collegial fashion while striving to do your personal best. If you work hard to develop the skills needed to be a good attorney, and if you apply sound techniques of exam writing, you likely will maximize your ability to get good grades while maintaining positive relationships. In turn, your ability to collaborate with others will help you maximize your performance in a law office, either in your first clerking job or after graduation.

B. Pace Yourself

You should view your work in the first semester as something of a long-distance race. Pace yourself so that you work steadily and effectively without falling behind, retaining a reserve of energy for a final kick at the end of the semester.

Gone are the days in college when you can coast during the semester, cram for the final exam, and then retain critical information just long enough to perform well on the examination. As you will soon see in subsequent chapters of this book, the knowledge that you acquire and the skills that you develop in the early weeks of the first semester of law school will lay the foundation for concepts introduced later in the semester. Consequently, your academic life in the second half of the semester will be more manageable if you take your studies seriously from the first day of class.

C. Walk into the Exam Room with the Confidence of a Winner

If all goes well, you will be so well prepared for your first set of exams that you will approach each exam with confidence, eager to show what you can do. A little nervous anxiety during the examination can be constructive, because it will help you focus your attention on the task at hand. With thorough preparation and some preexamination motivational techniques, you can manage that nervous energy and channel it into productive and disciplined exam writing.

II. SUBSTANCE: A PLAN OF ACTION

Success in law school examinations does not come solely from exposure to information about examination techniques. It comes largely from effective study habits throughout the semester, a thorough understanding of the nature of law school examinations, and hours of honing your skills with problems and practice exams.

A. Effective Study Habits

This book recommends and describes a three-part process for success in developing the knowledge and skills necessary for good performance on law school examinations. First, it describes the tasks of reading and interpreting statutes and the published decisions of courts, the latter of which are commonly referred to as *cases*. Second, it discusses the process of "synthesizing" cases, through which you will compare and contrast the facts, outcomes, and reasoning of cases that address similar legal questions. Third, it explains how to create study guides for exams, such as course outlines, checklists, and flowcharts.

B. Gaining Comfort with Uncertainty

You will learn many fundamental rules in law school and will discover that some simple legal questions have certain answers. The legal questions that your professor likely will find to be most interesting, however, both in class and on examinations, are ones that have no certain answer. The answer may be uncertain because the content of the applicable rule is subject to debate. Alternatively, even if the content of the rule is settled, it may be unclear whether the particular facts of a new case satisfy the requirements of the rule.

With respect to questions of this nature, this book demonstrates that your task is not to identify the "correct" answer (because there is no single and certain answer), but to identify the issue and the possible outcomes, while articulating the competing arguments that support each of the potential outcomes. The sooner that you become comfortable confronting and analyzing questions with answers that are uncertain, the sooner you will make progress in your study of the law.

C. Exam Preparation

In addition to learning the law and developing analytic skills, you must develop expertise with the examination process through which law professors will assess your knowledge and skills. This book describes in detail various types of law exam questions, and it describes several ways to develop your examination skills at several stages in the first semester.

D. Examination Techniques

Diligent preparation throughout the semester will translate into good exam performance only if you apply effective examination techniques, such as these:

(1) Allocate your time wisely during an exam;
(2) Take care to thoroughly understand the facts of a question and the call of the question; and
(3) Effectively identify issues and writing complete answers that display sound reasoning rather than a tendency to jump to conclusions.

This book examines these and other exam techniques in great detail.

III. THE NEXT STEP

Now that you have your roadmap, it is time to turn to Chapter 2 for a preview of your destination: law school exams in various formats. If you understand the nature of law school examinations, you will read the succeeding chapters on exam preparation with greater appreciation and comprehension.

Overview: Types of Examinations

You will better appreciate the discussions of study skills in the next few chapters if you first have a general idea of the nature of law school examinations. Accordingly, this chapter provides you with a quick overview of the most common types of examinations that you will encounter in law school. A much more detailed discussion of exams awaits you in Part IV.

I. FACT-BASED ESSAY EXAMINATIONS IN IRAC FORMAT

The most common type of essay examination is one that tells a story and then asks the test-taker to analyze the legal significance of the described events. For example, an essay exam in a Criminal Law course could describe fictitious events in several paragraphs and then ask students to discuss the crimes that might have been committed, as well as the defenses to those crimes. Sometimes the specific query at the end of the exam question—the "call of the question"—will limit the scope of the test-taker's analysis by asking for discussion only of certain issues, such as only those crimes committed by particular characters in the story, or only certain kinds of crimes or defenses.

The test-taker usually is expected to explore such an essay question in the framework of a deductive argument. In legal analysis, you can remember the elements of such an argument with the acronym IRAC, which stands for *issue, rule, application* (or analysis of facts), and *conclusion*:

Issue: Identify each legal issue that is raised by the facts.
Rule: For each issue, summarize the legal rule that would apply to help resolve the issue or summarize the competing legal rules that different courts or legislatures have adopted.

Application: Apply the law to the facts to determine whether the applicable legal rule is satisfied.

Conclusion: Reach a reasonable conclusion.

Within this model, essay questions can still differ in various ways. The next sections discuss the difference between an essay question that invites arguments for both sides of the dispute and one in which the analysis of each issue leads to a single, correct conclusion.

A. Arguments for Both Sides in the Face of Uncertainty

1. Close Questions with Uncertain Answers

The most interesting legal questions present close questions for the courts, so that neither the parties nor their attorneys are able to predict how a court will interpret or develop the law, or how a jury will apply the law to the facts. Accordingly, as discussed in detail in Chapter 10, many professors prefer to raise issues for which there is no single, certain conclusion to each issue. You will earn the most points on such issues by discussing arguments for both sides of the dispute, arguments that support competing conclusions.

2. An Illustration in a Nonlegal Context

To illustrate this analytic process with a metaphor from a nonlegal setting, imagine two basketball teams competing for the national championship, which will be awarded to the team that first wins four games. For example, as I wrote this chapter for the first edition, the Miami Heat and the Dallas Mavericks were set to begin competing for the 2006 National Basketball Association championship. If someone had asked me "Which team will win the series?" I would have been forced to admit that I could not be certain of the outcome of the series, just as an attorney cannot be certain how a court will rule in a close case that is pending before it. Nonetheless, I could analyze this issue in the following way: I could develop some rules or standards for assessing the strength of basketball teams, I could apply those standards to the facts while developing and weighing arguments for both teams, and I could identify a conclusion by making my best prediction about which team will win.

Thus, I might identify some reasonable multifaceted rule for assessing basketball teams in the playoffs, such as the following fictitious one, which I will pretend was published in a leading sports magazine:

> A team likely will win a playoff game if it is superior to its opponent on the basis of a balancing of the following factors: (a) quality of coaching; (b) presence of

dominating or star players; (c) ability to work together as a team; (d) health or injury status of important players; (e) the depth of the bench, in the sense of the quality of nonstarting players; (f) whether the team has home court advantage based on its total win-loss record during the regular season; and (g) how these two playoff teams match up against each other, based on such things as whether one team's style of offense is particularly difficult for the other team to defend against.

If this is the only highly respected standard for assessing a team's likelihood of winning, I would simply summarize it as the applicable rule and then move to the next step: applying the branches or elements of the rule to the facts of the Miami Heat and Dallas Mavericks. Especially if the question provided a rich set of facts for analysis, I would probably discuss each numbered element separately, treating it as a subissue. Thus, for each element for which relevant facts are provided, I would apply that element of the rule to those facts, and reach a conclusion.

For example, in applying element (a) to the teams as they were constituted in 2006, I might compare the many years of experience of the Miami Heat coach, Pat Riley—who coached the Los Angeles Lakers to four league championships many years earlier—with the bright new talent shown by the Dallas Mavericks coach, Avery Johnson, who won NBA Coach of the Year honors in his first full season of coaching just before these playoff games. Although I undoubtedly would have my own opinion about which coach is superior, my analysis would be most complete and helpful if I recognized that many sports enthusiasts will differ on these questions. Consequently, I would present arguments for both sides of this debate by describing the strengths and weaknesses of each coach. Although neither conclusion on this subissue is the single "correct" one, I would make a judgment about which arguments are more compelling and would state a subsidiary conclusion on this element.

In applying element (b) to the team rosters as they stood for the playoff games in 2006, I might discuss whether star players for the Miami Heat, such as Shaquille O'Neil and Dwyane Wade, or star players for the Dallas Mavericks, such as Dirk Nowitzky and Jason Terry or Jerry Stackhouse, are likely to control the action when they are on the court. Again, I would present both sides of these arguments, such as describing the strengths and weaknesses of each star under consideration, and reach a conclusion on this subissue.

In this fashion, I would apply each element of the rule for which I had relevant facts, arguing both sides as I go, and reach subsidiary conclusions. On the basis of my analyses of all these elements, I would then make my best judgment about which team appears to have the best overall chance of success, and I would make a prediction about which team will win.

Of course, no one could know for certain which team would win until the series had been fully played,[1] just as no one can be sure of the outcome of a novel legal question until the highest appellate court in the relevant jurisdiction has accepted that question for review and issued its decision. Consequently, your examiner will not care which conclusion you reach on a close question, but will be impressed if you have thoughtfully applied the pertinent standards to relevant facts and have demonstrated that you can present arguments supporting either conclusion.

To be sure, legal questions will be decided differently than athletic contests. Nonetheless, the basketball metaphor serves to illustrate the process of fully analyzing a question for which there is no certain answer, including presenting arguments that support either of two potential conclusions. In a law school examination, such a question often is formed when the examiner provides facts that are close to the line between satisfying or not satisfying a legal rule and when the test-taker can use different facts (or occasionally, the same facts) to support opposite conclusions.

3. Depth of Analysis and Time Pressure

You can imagine that the multifaceted analysis just described will take some time to plan and express. Even if it were not joined with other issues, the subissues of the single question about which basketball team would prevail in the playoffs could occupy a test-taker for 45 minutes in a classroom, or even several hours if developed into a more formal memo in a take-home examination.

The depth of analysis that is possible will depend on the richness of the facts provided to the test-taker and the time permitted for the exam answer. In most cases, students take law school exams together in a classroom, with time limits that produce intense time pressure. Indeed, some exams, often referred to as *issue-spotting exams*, present facts that raise so many legal issues that test-takers might have time only to identify the most important issues and to provide a hurried reference to the law and the facts of each. In contrast, a take-home exam, or an in-class exam with substantial time allotted for a manageable number of issues, permits test-takers to analyze the facts in greater detail and to more conscientiously argue both sides of the dispute.

---

1. As it turned out, the Dallas Mavericks won the first two games of the series, but the Miami Heat won the series by winning the next four games, with the Miami Heat stars, especially Dwyane Wade, dominating at critical times. *See* Liz Robbins, "Heat Claims Its First Championship," N.Y. Times, June 20, 2006, at D1. This outcome, however, was not predictable with any certainty before the series started, and certainly not after the first two games were played.

B. Emphasizing the Process of Reaching a Correct Conclusion

1. A Full Analysis Still Earns the Most Points

As discussed in detail in Chapter 11, some essay examinations will invite a full analysis in IRAC form but will nonetheless raise at least one issue that the examiner believes leads to a single correct conclusion, because settled rules apply to the facts in a predictable way. In such an exam, it should not be important for you to present competing arguments, and the examiner presumably will reward you in some way for identifying the correct conclusion. Nonetheless, the examiner will still be more interested in the process by which you reach your conclusion than in the conclusion itself. In other words, you will still earn most of your points with an informative description of the rule and a thoughtful and thorough application of the rule to the facts.

2. An Illustration in a Nonlegal Context

For example, imagine that an examination asks you to fully discuss whether an average person would express pain, through verbal exclamation or physical reaction, if the person's bare hand momentarily brushed against a hot baking pan that had just been removed from an oven that was heated to 400 degrees. From experience, you would undoubtedly conclude that the correct answer is "yes." Nonetheless, you might also be aware that your examiner expects you to know and to explain in detail the physiological factors that would cause the person to feel sufficient pain to react audibly or visibly.

In your explanation, you might identify two issues or topics for discussion: (1) the transfer of information to the brain about the temperature of the pan, and (2) the body's reaction to that information. For your first IRAC, you would summarize the scientific knowledge about how nerves in the hand send pain signals to the brain in certain kinds of circumstances (a rule about how the body operates), and you would apply that rule to the facts to conclude that the brain would receive a strong stimulus that would be interpreted as sharp pain. In a separate IRAC framework, you would then summarize information about involuntary physical reactions that would be prompted by the brain in response to such signals in an average person (more rules). You would then apply these rules to the facts of your case, and you would undoubtedly conclude that an average person who touches a hot baking pan with a bare hand would emit a cry of pain or at least would urgently withdraw the hand.

Law school essay questions of this nature usually invite application of a complicated set of legal rules to facts, raising interesting questions about the interrelationship of legal rules rather than about uncertainty in the application of the rules to the facts. In light of the certainty of the rules and the uncontroversial manner in which the rules apply to relevant facts, the analysis should lead to a particular conclusion. Nonetheless, an examiner will typically award most of the possible points to answers that identify the correct rules and apply them to the facts in a complete, orderly, and logical fashion.

3. Advocating for One Side of the Dispute

Occasionally, an exam question will present facts that raise a close issue with no certain answer, but the call of the question identifies one party as your client, on whose behalf you should argue. If the exam says no more, you generally should interpret this instruction as inviting arguments for both sides on all issues, because—as in an office memorandum assignment—you should explore the weaknesses as well as the strengths of your client's arguments.

In very rare cases, however, the question will ask you to present only the arguments for one side, as you might when advocating for one of the parties in a brief to a court. In response to such a question, you would not argue both sides of the dispute in a balanced fashion, even if the question is a close one, because you are playing the role of advocate for one side only.

II. ESSAY QUESTIONS REQUIRING DISCUSSION OTHER THAN IN FULL IRAC FORMAT

Some essay questions will ask for a discussion that is more focused or limited than the full deductive reasoning associated with the IRAC format, such as one that asks you to explain a legal rule or to discuss the policies supporting or opposing a rule or proposed rule. Although these are not as common as traditional fact-based essay exams requesting both legal and factual discussion, essay questions might come in a wide variety of formats, so it is important that you read the directions of the question carefully and follow them precisely.

III. OBJECTIVE QUESTIONS: TRUE–FALSE AND MULTIPLE-CHOICE QUESTIONS

At least a portion of many law school exams are commonly characterized as objective in nature, in the sense that your responses on a "bubble sheet" can be graded by a scanner and do not require the examiner to apply his or her judgment to assess the quality of your answer.

A simple example is a true–false test, which sets forth sequentially numbered statements and asks you to identify each statement as true or false. More common are multiple-choice questions with four or five alternative responses, only one of which is correct, or—much less commonly—only one of which is incorrect. In either case, a question might require you to assess the accuracy of a statement or statements about legal rules. Alternatively, the question might present a set of facts, much like those in an essay question, and ask you to assess the accuracy of a statement or statements about the law and how it applies to the facts.

Because true–false and multiple-choice questions must draw sharp lines between correct and incorrect responses, they often call for a more sophisticated and precise knowledge of legal rules than do essay questions. Moreover, although essay questions also demand a high level of reading comprehension, true–false and multiple-choice questions frequently require particularly careful and critical reading, because a seemingly innocuous word or phrase might create a falsehood that eliminates the response as a true or correct one.

IV. THE NEXT STEP

Now that you have a general picture of law school exams, you probably have surmised that you must develop an effective plan for preparing for them. To perform well on essay exams, you must learn difficult legal concepts, memorize many key points of law, and develop your skills of analysis and expression. Turn now to Part II, which presents strategies for effective exam preparation.

PART TWO

LAW SCHOOL STUDY TECHNIQUES

Most law students experience "grade shock" when they realize that all the members of their entering class earned As in college but that only a small percentage of them can claim a place at the top of the demanding grading curve mandated at most law schools. Many law students simply underestimate the level of academic performance invited by the exams and the intellectual strengths and studious habits of their classmates.

Chapters 3 and 4 consist partly of a pep talk on the virtues of discipline, hard work, and effective use of your time. This might come off as a little corny or preachy, but it might also provide the best advice you receive upon entering law school.

CHAPTER 3

Getting Ready for Law School

Your preparation for law school exams should begin even before the first day of class. Careful planning will help you lay a foundation for progress throughout the semester leading up to exams.

I. THE IMPORTANCE OF ATTITUDE

A. Take Your Studies Seriously

If you applied good study habits in college, and took care to analyze, organize, and express complex information in college term papers, you are well prepared for the challenges of studying the law. On the other hand, if you breezed through college without a disciplined study routine, cramming for exams at the last minute while still managing to convey sufficient information to earn high grades, you are obviously bright and resourceful, but you can only hope that you are bright enough to grasp that those habits will not serve you well in law school.

It is true that a few upper division law students will delight in telling you that they rarely opened the casebook for a course, seldom attended class, surfed the Internet through most of the classes they did attend, and still managed to earn a passing grade by studying a commercial outline of the course a few days before the exam. When you hear such stories, you should take them with a large grain of salt. Some upper division students have a tendency to exaggerate the extent to which they were able to "beat the system," because reciting such stories makes them feel "cool" and clever. In contrast, if you observe the habits of most successful law students, you will see that they organize their time carefully, study conscientiously throughout the semester, discuss course material with members of their study group, and work with assigned legal material in ways that develop lasting skills.

Of course, as a law professor, I must consider the possibility that I preach the values of conscientious study habits with excessive zeal, especially because I am forced to admit that hard work in law school will not always translate to top grades and will not address every skill and personal characteristic that is important to lawyering. Still, it seems irrational for you to do anything but commit to the most ambitious study habits possible in law school, for the following reasons:

- Your grades, and the opportunities on which grades are based, will be defined on a demanding curve in most law schools, and most of your classmates will be highly motivated, academically well prepared, and diligent. You will want to develop the capacity to run with this crowd and study effectively with them, rather than let them pass you by while you spend excessive time in front of the TV or at the local pub.
- By studying conscientiously, you will develop skills that will not only maximize your chances of scoring well on exams, but also will help you work effectively in your first job at a law firm, where you will be called on to research and analyze law that you have never studied and will not find in a commercial outline.
- When a good law school accepted you into its entering class, you acquired a scarce and highly coveted opportunity denied to many others. After acquiring such an opportunity and paying substantial tuition for your training, it is difficult to justify any course of action other than doing your very best.

B. But Put a Positive Spin on It

Okay, let's assume that I have persuaded you to prepare for law school exams by studying conscientiously throughout the semester. To clarify, I am not advocating that you elevate the stress in your life to counter-productive levels. Just as successful lawyers derive maximum satisfaction by striking a healthy balance in their lives, you will do your best in law school if you are able to maintain good physical and emotional health, continue to nurture important relationships, and study diligently because you take pride in your work and enjoy the progress that you are making.

Notice that I mentioned enjoyment. To some extent, the ultimate measure of your success in law school is the extent to which you are positively motivated to work hard because you enjoy the intellectual stimulation, the academic challenges, and the sense of accomplishment when you have an "a-ha" moment as some elusive concept comes into focus. If this sense of academic enjoyment does not come naturally, you might try to devise ways to appreciate the intellectual challenges of your studies.

Only you can identify the techniques that will enable you to bring a positive attitude to the study of law. Remember, however, that enjoyment of a challenging task is sometimes partly a matter of consciously deciding to see the positive side of an activity rather than dwelling on the negative. To illustrate, have you ever found yourself walking along a sidewalk, sulking over some minor setback, only to be struck by the realization that it is a beautiful day, you are passing by trees and shrubs that are blooming, and you are lucky to be alive to enjoy these sensations? If you then convince yourself to change your scowl to a smile, you sometimes can consciously transform a negative outlook to a more positive one. Similarly, if you find yourself dreading your class preparation or participation, try to consciously put a smile on your face by remembering the value of your scarce seat in law school, the opportunities that it represents, the marketable skills that hard work will bring, and the ways in which you will be able to apply those skills to assist clients and the community.

II. HIT THE GROUND RUNNING

Before your first semester of law school begins, you should get your life fully in order so that you are ready to immerse yourself in your studies without reservation or distraction. Move into your new apartment, secure your finances, express your heartfelt gratitude to family members or your significant other for patience and support, and leave time for a relaxing, mind-clearing week before the first day of class. Get the most out of your school's orientation session, and remember that most law professors will assign readings for the first day of class.

For most students, terminating even part-time employment is an essential step in preparing for law school, because law schools expect students to immerse themselves completely in their studies during the first year of law school. Therefore, rather than work substantial hours during your first year of law school, save for law school in the preceding years, and apply for every scholarship for which you are eligible. If you must work during the first year, you are a good candidate for a part-time law school program, if one is available to you, which would allow you to spread your studies over a greater number of semesters.

Still, if the only educational program available to you is a full-time program, and if you must work or if you have substantial family obligations, all is not lost. Sometimes the busiest people can manage multiple obligations through skillfully organizing their time and cutting all waste from their schedules. The discussion in the next section will help you assess whether you can handle the workload of law school while assuming other important responsibilities.

III. ORGANIZE AND USE YOUR TIME WISELY

A. Prepare a Schedule

One of your most important tasks before classes begin is to create a weekly schedule of activities that helps you organize your time efficiently. Your schedule will obviously depend on your personal circumstances. Nonetheless, the following tips might be helpful to most students.

- *Set aside time to prepare for each class.* Many law students find that they need to set aside two to three hours to prepare for each hour of class. If you meet in class for 15 hours each week, you can easily spend 30 to 45 hours each week reading assigned materials and preparing written case briefs. When this commitment is added to the time spent in class, you are already spending 45 to 60 hours each week immersed in the law. Create a weekly schedule that identifies the hours each day, including weekends for most students, during which you will prepare for class.
- *Set aside time for other assigned schoolwork.* In addition to class preparation, you will be spending time reviewing course material alone or in study groups, drafting course outlines in preparation for exams, writing legal memoranda for one or more courses, attending special public seminars featuring guest speakers, meeting with your professors during office hours, participating in student organizations and community service, and posting questions or responses on an Internet component of one or more of your courses. If you are called on to participate in several of these activities in a single week, you might be forced to slice into the time you have set aside for class preparation. Set aside some extra time in your schedule, however, for these additional activities so that you can minimize encroachment on your class preparation time.

   If you must also devote time in your schedule to employment or family responsibilities, you likely will need to borrow some hours from all of the academic tasks just described. You can do this by sacrificing some desirable but nonmandatory law school activities, such as public seminars and student organization meetings, and by reducing your study time and compensating for the reduced time with particularly intense concentration.
- *Make room for your studies and make the most of your time.* It must be obvious by now that the study of law, as well as the practice of law, will require you to lead a fairly disciplined life, with a minimum of wasted time. This is not such a bad thing; a brisk, full, well-organized life can be much more satisfying than one lacking any objectives that would motivate you to engage in productive activity. Moreover, I am not suggesting that you sacrifice things that are important to your life and well-being, such as activities with family or a partner; rest and exercise; and meditation, reflection, or spirituality. You should be

prepared, however, to bid farewell to excessive hours in front of the television, playing computer games, or drinking at your favorite bar.

To optimize your precious time, make effective use of minutes that might otherwise be wasted. If you expect to wait an hour at the doctor's office before being called for your appointment, bring some of your assigned reading with you. You will pass the time much more quickly, and with less anxiety, than if you were staring at the clock and worrying about the reading awaiting you at home.

When unanticipated circumstances upset the most carefully planned schedule, however, or if you are simply unable to read another page, give yourself a break without wallowing in guilt. An occasional unscheduled break for a bit of exercise or a musical interlude might enable you to return to your work with increased productivity.

B. Use Class Time to Your Advantage

One obvious way to make effective use of time might be the most difficult to implement. Consider this: You probably have taken on significant debt to pay tuition for law school while foregoing the opportunity to earn a salary in a full-time job; as a consequence, rather than punch the clock at a workplace each weekday, you are now required by school policy to attend classes regularly, where you will receive the benefits of those tuition dollars.

In light of this, it would be incredibly wasteful to "tune out" during class. After all, because you have paid for the scarce and valuable commodity of a seat in that class, and because you are required to attend class, you have every incentive to be as actively engaged in the class proceedings as possible, so that you can make the maximum amount of intellectual progress in class, thus increasing the efficiency of your study and review outside of class.

Here are some ideas for getting the most out of class discussion:

- *Be an engaged, active listener.* If the professor has directed a question to another student, pretend that the question has been put to you, and formulate your response, in writing in your notes if you have time. Be ready at a moment's notice to take over for the other student without missing a beat, in case the professor shifts his or her attention to you.

  Listen carefully to the professor's comments, legal terminology, and style of questions. These might provide verbal clues to the kinds of questions likely to appear on the exam or the kinds of exam answers that the professor will value.

- *Do not be afraid to ask questions or share ideas.* Do not ask tangential questions or make self-serving observations just to show off; respect the needs of your classmates by making contributions to class discussion that advance the education for everyone. On the other hand, do not shy away from asking for a clarification out of a misplaced fear of sounding dim-witted; if you are well prepared and have been paying attention, it is much more likely that many other students are sharing your confusion and will be grateful if someone asks for further discussion on a topic. If you remain confused about an area of law after studying diligently for class, reviewing your notes, and seeking clarification in study groups, make an appointment to visit your professor during office hours, or post your question on the discussion forum of the Internet component of your course.

- *Take effective notes.* If you have prepared well for class, you will already have a substantial set of notes that summarizes assigned cases and other text. You can then supplement your class preparation notes by writing down during class discussion further points and questions that strike you as being significant.

  During class, avoid taking verbatim dictation of every word spoken by the professor, even if your use of a laptop computer enables and encourages you to do so; the resulting notes will be too voluminous and insufficiently selective to be useful to you later. Instead, summon your intellectual energies for the demanding tasks of listening, thinking, and making mental connections in class, allowing you to record points, questions, or conclusions that you judge to be significant. Then, take some time after class to review your notes, to fill in gaps in the notes, and sometimes even to strike out superfluous or confused passages, while the discussion is fresh in your mind.

IV. THE NEXT STEP

By now you have had an earful of my preaching the virtues of discipline, organization, and active engagement in class. It is time for more specific instructions about study techniques. Turn to the next chapter for directions on briefing cases and for advice on confronting uncertainty in the law.

CHAPTER 4

Class Preparation and Participation

To prepare well for law school examinations, you must assimilate an enormous amount of complicated legal material, become comfortable with uncertainty in legal questions, learn to analyze the legal significance of facts, and display impressive skills of organization and written expression. This chapter and the next describe study techniques that will help you meet these academic challenges.

I. INTRODUCTION TO THE LEGAL SYSTEM

A. Branches of Government

A brief introduction to our legal system will help you appreciate the discussions that follow about class preparation and participation. Our introduction begins with federal and state constitutions as the bedrock statements of governing principles in the federal and state systems of government within the United States. A fundamental principle shared by those constitutions is the division of government into three branches: the executive, legislative, and judicial.

Executive officials, such as the U.S. President or a state governor, may propose legislation, and administrative agencies within the executive branch may create administrative rules or regulations that help implement a statutory scheme. For the most part, however, the executive branch is responsible for enforcing laws rather than making them.

B. Legislation

Congress and the state legislatures are the primary sources of lawmaking in the federal and state legal systems. As elected officials, legislators create law in the form of legislation, by enacting statutes. The judicial branch helps to implement legislation, because judges interpret and apply statutes to particular disputes. For example, a criminal statute might provide that a robber must "use a weapon" to be guilty of the elevated crime of aggravated robbery. A court might provide further definition to this statutory text by deciding in a criminal case that a bank robber who brandished a realistic toy gun satisfied this statutory requirement. In turn, the legislature can supersede a judicial interpretation of a statute by enacting an amendment to the statute, such as by amending the aggravated robbery statute to define "weapon" in a way that excludes toys that could not cause serious harm.

C. Common Law

When courts interpret and apply statutes, it is a matter of some debate whether they are simply following the law that the legislature has created, or whether they are making law by filling gaps in the statute or interpreting ambiguous statutory terms. As a practical matter, judicial interpretation of statutes undeniably affects the extent to which the law applies to actual disputes, so judicial interpretations do indeed help define the breadth and reach of statutory law.

Moreover, no one disputes that judges create law when they develop and refine the rules of a separate body of law known as the *common law.* For centuries in England, in the United States, and in other common law countries, when a constitutional or statutory provision has not comprehensively applied to a legal dispute, the courts have developed and applied their own rules of common law, which are based on custom, policy, and common sense. Much of state tort law and contract law, for example, is still governed by common law, which the courts continue to develop and adapt to changing societal needs.

Courts develop common law rules incrementally, as they decide particular disputes, with each decision representing another brick in the structure of the common law.

Just as a legislature can enact new legislation overruling a judicial interpretation of an existing statute, it can also displace a rule of the common law. With regard to the contract law that applies to sales of goods, for example, state legislatures have replaced many of the common law rules with legislation, in the form of commercial codes, or cohesive collections of related statutory provisions. To return to the metaphor of the common law as a brick structure, the intervention of legislation would cover up part of a wall of the common law structure with a legislative layer of concrete.

This new legislative structure has some gaps in it, where the common law bricks show through spaces in the concrete, so even sales of goods are governed by a combination of statutory provisions and common law.

Moreover, because this new structure applies only to sales of goods, other kinds of contracts, such as contracts for real estate or personal services, are still largely governed by the common law structure, the bricks of which are displaced only in spots by occasional statutory trimming.

Whenever a court interprets a statute, we might imagine that the court's decision sculpts and further defines the surface of the statutory concrete that had displaced common law brick.

If the legislature disagrees with a court's interpretation of a statute, it can modify the statute or replace the statute with a new one, clarifying the legislature's intent and smoothing over the etching of the judicial interpretation.

D. Case Law and Cases

Because a judicial decision might be interpreting a statute or other enacted law rather than developing and applying common law, a judicial decision does not always represent common law. It will thus be helpful to use a more general term, *case law,* to refer to the law that is established when a court issues a judicial opinion. Some case law will interpret statutory or constitutional law, some will further develop and apply common law, and some will do both.

In the broadest sense, a *case* in law school could be a real or hypothetical event that gives rise to a legal dispute, such as a customer slipping, falling, and suffering injuries in a pool of spilled vegetable oil in a grocery store, arguably resulting from the store's negligent failure to clean the spill more quickly. More narrowly, law students and professors regularly use the term *case* as shorthand for a judicial decision that resolves a dispute and presents case law in a printed judicial opinion. You will most often study law from a *casebook,* which collects hundreds of these cases—these judicial opinions—and organizes them by topic.

Following is an example of a fictitious case, purposely composed to be shorter and simpler than most of those appearing in your casebooks, so that it does not distract us too long from our overview of the legal system.

Comco, Inc. v. Sterling Mfg.
Supreme Court of New Maine (2010)

Opinion of the Court by Grant, J.:

Comco, Inc. ("Comco") brought an action for breach of a sales contract against Sterling Manufacturing ("Sterling"). The trial court granted Sterling's motion to dismiss, which the Court of Appeals affirmed. We now affirm.

FACTS

On review of a motion to dismiss, we must assume the truth of Comco's allegations and draw factual inferences in its favor, just as a jury might. *Dunn v. Gale,* 271 N. Me. 61, 62 (1956). The complaint alleges the following:

Sterling mailed a purchase order on June 11, 2007, for six units of factory machinery manufactured and supplied by Comco. The purchase order referred to Comco's current catalog in describing the machinery and in specifying the prices, totaling $2,000,000; it required delivery within two weeks; and it stated Sterling's willingness to pay on delivery. On June 13, after receiving the purchase order, Comco sent a fax to Sterling, stating: "Thank you for your purchase order of June 11. We will give it our prompt attention." Two days later, Sterling telephoned Comco to revoke its offer. Comco insisted that it had already accepted Sterling's offer and that the parties were bound by contract. Sterling refused to take delivery of the machinery or pay for it.

PROCEEDINGS IN THE COURTS BELOW

Comco sued for breach of contract, alleging lost profits. Sterling moved to dismiss the complaint. In its motion to dismiss, Sterling admitted that its purchase order constituted an offer, but it argued that Comco's admitted response to the offer was too ambiguous to constitute an acceptance, and that Sterling consequently revoked its offer before Comco accepted. The trial court agreed and granted Sterling's motion to dismiss. The Court of Appeals affirmed. Comco here argues that the trial court and the Court of Appeals erred in denying it the opportunity to prove that its admitted response to the offer was an unequivocal expression of assent. We reject this contention and accordingly affirm the judgment of the Court of Appeals.

ANALYSIS

We will approve dismissal of a complaint only if it appears that the plaintiff cannot prove any set of facts that would entitle him to relief on his claim. *Dunn*, 271 N. Me. at 62. Thus, in this case, we must determine whether Comco might establish some context in which its response to the purchase order would be interpreted as conveying an acceptance.

Because this is a transaction in goods, the issue of contract formation is governed by Article 2 of the New Maine Commercial Code, N. Me. Com. C. § 2-102, as interpreted in our case law. Under that code, "[a] contract for the sale of goods may be made in any manner sufficient to show agreement." *Id.* § 2-204(1). Nonetheless, an ambiguous response to an offer is not sufficient to show agreement; at the least, an acceptance requires a definite and unambiguous expression of assent, so that the parties have a reliable basis on which to determine whether they are contractually bound. *See id.* § 2-207(1) (requiring a definite expression of acceptance to create a contract on conflicting forms); *Bales v. Scott*, 182 N. Me. 2d 432 (1991) (interpreting N. Me. Comm. C. § 2-204(1)). In *Bales*, for example, we held that an offeree did not express acceptance when she stated that she would "give this generous offer the serious consideration that it deserves." *Id.* at 435.

In this case, Comco asserts that its statement that it would give "prompt attention" to Sterling's purchase order meant that it was accepting the order and was promptly making preparations to ship the equipment. That is one possible interpretation of Comco's response; however, Comco's words are hardly a definite and unambiguous expression of assent. The response is equally consistent with an apparent intention to check existing stock or to check for price increases before accepting or rejecting the offer. Because the response thus conveyed with equal force either an acceptance of the offer or a desire to further consider the offer, it could not constitute an acceptance.

We cannot conceive of any plausible set of facts with which Comco could persuade a jury that its admitted response definitely and unambiguously expressed acceptance. The trial court thus properly dismissed the complaint.

Accordingly, we affirm.

Dissent by ROBERTS, J.:

It is entirely possible to conceive of factual contexts in which a reasonable offeror in Sterling's position would interpret Comco's response as unambiguously expressing assent. I therefore would reverse and allow this case to proceed for further fact-finding, if not in a full trial, at least on a record developed for a motion for summary judgment. Accordingly, I dissent from the majority's opinion.

E. Court Structure

Aside from minor courts of limited jurisdiction, the federal court system and the court systems in most states are organized in a three-tiered structure: Lawsuits are brought in a trial court, named the *Superior Court* in many states, and the *District Court* in the federal system. The trial court hears the evidence and renders a judgment, sometimes after a jury finds the facts. The losing party then has the right to appeal that decision to an intermediate appellate court. Finally, the party who loses in the intermediate appellate court can seek further review in the highest court, sometimes referred to as the *court of last resort* (named the *Supreme Court* in the federal system and in most state systems). A few state systems have no intermediate appellate court, but the following federal courts, which show the progression from trial court to court of last resort, illustrate the more common three-tiered model:

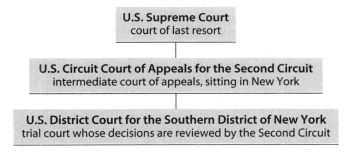

U.S. Supreme Court
court of last resort

U.S. Circuit Court of Appeals for the Second Circuit
intermediate court of appeals, sitting in New York

U.S. District Court for the Southern District of New York
trial court whose decisions are reviewed by the Second Circuit

Although a few cases in your casebooks might be decisions of federal district courts, the vast majority will be published opinions of state or federal appellate courts, either intermediate appellate courts or courts of last resort. These cases, these published opinions, form *precedent*, which can control or influence the outcome of future decisions under a doctrine known as *stare decisis*.

F. Precedent and Stare Decisis

1. Binding Precedent

To varying degrees, the doctrine of stare decisis commands courts to follow the examples set by previous decisions. To return to the earlier metaphor of the judicial decisions as bricks in a growing structure, previous decisions of a court provide a foundation on which it and other courts below it can continue to build in a consistent manner.

Under the strongest application of stare decisis, a trial court or intermediate appellate court must follow the decisions—the precedent—of a higher court within its court system, a court that is in line to review its judgments. Refer to the earlier illustration of the federal court system, for example, and imagine that a federal trial court (the U.S. District Court) within the Second Circuit is applying precedent either of the U.S. Court of Appeals for the Second Circuit or of the U.S. Supreme Court. If the precedent is indistinguishable in its issues and material facts from the new dispute before the trial court, the precedent would be *binding*, because the District Court would be required by stare decisis to apply the precedent and reach the result dictated by the precedent.

2. Overruling a Court's Own Precedent in Special Circumstances

An appellate court can overrule *its own precedent* and can replace it with a new view of the law. Under stare decisis, however, the court will do so only if it has very good reason to depart from its decision in a previous case, such as changed circumstances in society or a realization that its precedent was wrongly decided or has turned out to be unworkable.

3. Precedent from Other Court Systems May Be Persuasive but Not Binding

A court is not bound at all by decisions of courts below it within the same system, nor is it bound by decisions from other court systems, and sometimes not by decisions from coequal courts within the same system. However, it might find the reasoning of the nonbinding decisions to be persuasive in developing its own rule. For example, the U.S. Court of Appeals for the Second Circuit, sitting in New York, will not be bound by precedent of the U.S. Court of Appeals for the Ninth Circuit, sitting in California; nor will any state court in Michigan be bound by a decision of any state court in Florida. Each of these courts, however, can draw guidance from the decisions of other courts.

4. Precedent from a Reviewing Court May Be Distinguishable, and Thus Nonbinding, Although Still Potentially Useful

Finally, even when a precedent might otherwise be binding because of its source, it will not control the outcome of a new case if the facts or issues of the precedent differ from those of the new case in a legally significant way.

To return to our earlier example, imagine that in Case 1 a state court of last resort decided that a bank robber's use of a realistic toy gun satisfied a criminal statute's requirement that "a weapon" be used in the commission of a robbery to elevate the crime to "aggravated robbery." In arriving at this decision, the court examined the text of the criminal statute, as well as published statements of legislative purpose, in an effort to interpret the criminal statute in a manner consistent with the legislature's likely intentions. The court reasoned that even a toy gun, if apparently real and brandished in a threatening way, could engender fear and possibly trigger a dangerous response, thus justifying elevation of the crime.

Imagine further that the intermediate court of appeals in that state is confronted a year later with the following question in Case 2: As a matter of statutory interpretation, did a bank robber "use a weapon" in the commission of the crime, thus elevating the crime to aggravated robbery, if he had a loaded handgun in his coat pocket, ready to be produced if necessary to obtain the money and make his getaway, but which the robber never showed or mentioned to anyone?

The precedent of Case 1, even though a decision of the highest court in the state, would not dictate the outcome in Case 2, because the facts and issues of the two cases differ in a way that is legally significant. True, the two cases require interpretation of the same statutory language. Moreover, the reasoning of Case 1 might help the intermediate court of appeals predict what the highest court would do in Case 2. Nonetheless, Case 1 will not dictate the outcome of Case 2 in a simple way. A robber's act of holding in reserve a real, loaded gun that is never revealed raises a different question of statutory interpretation than a robber's act of brandishing a realistic toy that cannot actually be discharged. Thus, the cases are sufficiently "distinguishable" to preclude Case 1 from being automatically binding on the intermediate court of appeals in Case 2, and the intermediate court of appeals is compelled to engage in legal analysis that goes beyond applying Case 1 in a simple manner.

Whether the combination of analogies and differences between the cases justifies different outcomes or the same outcome will be a matter for the attorneys to argue before the intermediate court of appeals and perhaps later to the highest court in the state. For example, in an attempt to distinguish the two cases, the attorney for the defendant bank robber might argue that the concealed weapon was not "used" in the robbery, because Case 1 emphasized the harm or reactions that are produced by brandishing a real or apparent weapon, and the concealed weapon in Case 2 never made an appearance to produce any harm or reaction. The state prosecutor, on the other hand, might argue that the two cases are analogous in that the robber in each case brought a real or apparent weapon as a means of facilitating the crime, because the concealed weapon in Case 2 gave the robber a sense of power and security that helped him put his plans into action.

The "answer" to the question raised in such a dispute, of course, is uncertain, because it is impossible to predict with certainty how the courts will interpret the statute, either by searching for legislative intent on a question never specifically contemplated by the legislature or by focusing more narrowly on the meaning of the statutory text. However, if the legislature is disappointed with the statutory interpretation of the courts of the state, it can clarify the law by amending the statute.

G. Summary of Terms and Concepts

Within the limits prescribed by the state and federal constitutions, legislatures make law by enacting statutes. In the context of resolving specific disputes brought before them, courts make or further develop law in at least two ways: (1) They interpret and apply statutory or constitutional law; and (2) they create, develop, and apply their own body of common law, which applies when statutory law has not displaced common law rules. In either of these methods of judicial development of law, courts create case law when they issue an opinion explaining their decision in a dispute. In legal education, these judicial opinions are commonly known as *cases*, although that term can be used more broadly to refer to any set of facts, real or hypothetical, that raises a legal dispute between parties.

Under our system of stare decisis, previous published decisions of appellate courts are viewed as precedent. Precedent can dictate or influence the outcome of subsequent disputes brought before the courts. Within a court system, the precedent of a higher court will dictate the outcome of a new case (and will thus be binding), if the new case is not distinguishable from the precedent in any legally significant way. A court is freer to abandon its *own* precedent, even if indistinguishable from the current dispute, but it will do so only in special circumstances warranting a change in the course of the court's case law.

A court is not bound by previous decisions from courts below it or by decisions from other court systems. However, such decisions might be persuasively reasoned and might thus provide helpful guidance in the new case.

Finally, a court is not bound by decisions that are distinguishable on their facts or issues. The court might nonetheless reach the same result in the new case, either because the same result is justified for different reasons than those compelling the result in the precedent, or because analogies between the two cases outweigh the distinguishing factors.

II. BRIEFING CASES

Armed with this introduction to the legal system, you should be ready to begin reading and analyzing cases. Your law school will probably require your attendance at an orientation program, in which you will learn to prepare for class discussion by creating a *brief,* or a summary, of each case. In your case brief, you will summarize important elements of a judicial opinion and express your interpretation of it, providing you with a solid basis for discussing the case in class.

A. A Popular Format for a Case Brief

Different professors might discuss cases in slightly different ways, thus leading you to brief cases differently for various classes. Generally speaking, however, you will want to include the following elements in a case brief:

(1) *Identify the case.* Write down the name of the case, which typically consists of the names of the adversary parties to the dispute, such as *Brown v. Board of Education.* Identify the court that issued the opinion as well as the date of the decision, such as U.S. Supreme Court (1954). If you learn to record the official citation to the opinion, you will also know where to find the opinion in the library, such as with *Brown v. Board of Education,* 347 U.S. 483 (1954).

(2) *Summarize the facts.* When courts decide cases, they are resolving disputes that arise out of concrete events. The judicial opinion that you are briefing typically summarizes the facts that were established at trial or alleged in the complaint filed by the party who brought the lawsuit. After reading and analyzing the entire case, record in your own words the facts that you believe were critically important to the court's resolution of the dispute.

For example, a case brief might show that a contract dispute is based on the following facts:

> Sterling Co. offered through a mailed purchase order to pay $2 million for specified factory machinery manufactured and supplied by Comco. Comco immediately responded by mail that it would give Sterling's purchase order its "prompt attention." Two days later, Sterling telephoned Comco to revoke its offer. Comco insisted that it had already accepted Sterling's offer and that the parties were bound by contract. Sterling refused to perform.

(3) *Summarize the procedural history.* Briefly describe the critical rulings in the court or courts below the one that issued the decision you are briefing. In addition, identify the legal errors that the appealing party contends took place in those proceedings. This summary of the procedural posture of the case might help you understand the issues and any restrictions on the appellate court's review of the decision below it.

The contract dispute described earlier, for example, might have the following procedural history:

> Comco sued for breach of contract, and Sterling moved to dismiss the complaint. The trial court granted Sterling's motion on the basis that Comco's admitted response to Sterling's offer was not an acceptance. The court of appeals affirmed, and Comco appealed to the state supreme court. Comco argues that it was entitled to an opportunity to prove that its response to the offer constituted an unequivocal expression of assent.

This statement of the procedural history shows that the appealing party believes that the trial court erred in its application of legal rules regarding acceptance of offers, which will help you formulate your statement of the issue on appeal. The procedural history also states that the trial court dismissed the action on the face of the complaint, which requires the court to assume the truth of the facts alleged in the complaint and to draw inferences in favor of the complaining party, the plaintiff. In such a case, as you likely will learn during class discussion, the appellate court can freely review whether the alleged facts state a claim under the law, without granting any special deference to the trial court's ruling. Although these insights might sound foreign to you at the moment, they illustrate that your statement of the procedural history could help you follow discussion of secondary points during class discussion.

(4) *State the issues.* The facts of a case might raise questions about the content of the legal rules that will apply to those facts, or about whether the facts satisfy the legal rule. These questions, which the court must answer to resolve the dispute before it, are known as the *issues* of the case. In some cases the court identifies the issues in its judicial opinion; in others, you must construct the issues yourself, drawing guidance from the arguments of the parties and other statements of the court. State the issues with specificity, incorporating critical facts, so that you precisely identify the nature of the question or questions addressed by the court. For example, rather than simply asking whether the parties "formed a contract," ask whether "under any plausible set of facts Comco could prove its claim that it definitely and unambiguously accepted Sterling's offer by stating that it would give 'prompt attention' to Sterling's purchase order."

(5) *State the holdings.* A *holding* is the court's answer to the question presented in an issue. If your statement of the issue is appropriately specific, a simple "yes" or "no" might suffice to state the holding. In some cases, however, you might be able to add a brief explanation of the answer, providing a preview to the reasoning of the court:

"No. Comco's response failed to express an unambiguous acceptance, thus justifying dismissal of Comco's suit."

(6) *Discuss the court's reasoning.* In a typical case, the court discusses the content of the legal rules that apply to help resolve each issue, and discusses how those rules apply to the relevant facts. It might also discuss policy considerations that helped guide the court in developing the content of the rules or the manner in which they apply to facts.

The source of the legal rules might be a provision of the federal or a state constitution, or a statute enacted by Congress or a state legislature, or the text of an administrative regulation promulgated by an administrative agency charged with implementing a statutory scheme. Alternatively, in the absence of any of these forms of enacted law, the court might be applying and further developing its own common law rules. Indeed, in the same case, the court might apply a combination of any of these sources of law, especially if more than one issue is adjudicated.

In your case brief, identify the source of law that the court is applying, identify any rules that it develops or applies and the policies on which it relies, and summarize the court's reasoning in its application of the law to the facts of the case before it, including any distinctions or analogies it finds in precedent.

(7) *Evaluate the case.* Your professor will expect you to read and think critically, and to develop the ability to persuade a judge to accept or reject the rules expressed by other courts based on the soundness of the reasoning expressed by the other courts in their judicial opinions. Thus, you should not feel bound to agree with the holding and reasoning of a case assigned for class. React honestly to a court's decision, and explain why you think the opinion makes sense or why you find it to be unpersuasive.

(8) *Synthesize the case with other cases that address the same issue.* The important process of case synthesis is discussed in much greater detail in the next chapter, as a bridge to outlining. A brief introduction here should suffice to get you started.

If you are briefing the second or third case in a series of cases that address the same general issue in different disputes and on different facts, compare the facts, reasoning, and holding of the current case with the previous cases in the series. In this way, you can make some sense out of seemingly divergent holdings and can gain a broader view of the law. For example, you might explain:

> In *Comco v. Sterling,* Comco's statement of an intent to give "prompt attention" to the purchase order was consistent with simply considering the offer further; in contrast, the offeree's statement in *Ayala v. Grey* that she would "promptly fill the order" unambiguously expressed an intent to accept the offer and commit to performance.

B. A Sample Case Brief

As a general example, and not as a pattern to follow mechanically, consider the following sample brief of the fictitious case presented in Section I.D. above.

Comco, Inc. v. Sterling Mfg., (N. Me. 2010), Casebook p. 322.

Facts (based on allegations of the complaint): Sterling offered through a mailed purchase order to pay $2 million for specified factory machinery manufactured and supplied by Comco. Comco immediately responded by mail that it would give Sterling's purchase order its "prompt attention." Sterling telephoned Comco to revoke its offer. Comco asserted that a contract was formed and demanded performance; Sterling refused to perform.

Procedural History: Comco sued for breach of contract, and Sterling moved to dismiss the complaint. The trial court granted Sterling's motion on the basis that Comco's response to Sterling's offer was not a definite and unambiguous expression of acceptance. The court of appeals affirmed, and Comco appealed to the state supreme court.

Issue: Could Comco prove under any set of facts that its commitment to give "prompt attention" to the purchase order constituted a definite and unambiguous expression of assent?

Holding: No (with one dissent). As a matter of law, Comco's response was too ambiguous to constitute an acceptance, so the trial court properly dismissed the complaint.

Reasoning: The Court relied on New Maine Comm. Code § 2-207(1), which in another context requires a "definite expression of acceptance," and on case law that interpreted § 2-104 as requiring unambiguous expression of assent for acceptance. It repeatedly used these standards in tandem, apparently adopting a general rule that a response to an offer is not an acceptance unless it is a definite and unambiguous expression of assent. As a matter of policy, the Court seemed to be concerned about providing a clear and reliable basis on which parties could determine whether they had entered into a binding contract.

Analogous precedent: The Court referred to its previous decision in *Scott v. Bales* that the following response to an offer did not express acceptance: "[I] will give this generous offer the serious consideration that it deserves."

Application to facts: The Court found that Comco's statement that it would "give prompt attention" to the purchase order was ambiguous at best, because it could be interpreted by Sterling as no more than a plan to promptly consider whether to accept or reject the offer. The court could not conceive of any set of facts with which Comco could prove that this statement definitely and unambiguously expressed assent. Therefore, the trial court properly dismissed the complaint.

Evaluation: I think the dissent has a point. Precisely how Sterling would reasonably interpret Comco's statement might depend on facts that would not normally be detailed in the complaint but could be developed on a fuller record. Even more than the statement in *Scott v. Bales*, Comco's response might be viewed as clearly stating the equivalent of "we agree," depending on such things as whether sellers in that industry customarily used the "prompt attention" phrase to mean that they were filling the order. I think dismissal on the face of the complaint may have been premature.

Synthesis: In this case, the majority found that Comco's commitment to give "prompt attention" to the purchase order was consistent with simply considering the offer further. An even stronger example of failure to accept an offer is found in *Scott v. Bales,* in which a statement of intent to "give serious consideration" to an offer did not express assent. In contrast, the offeree's statement in *Ayala v. Grey* that she would "promptly fill the order" unequivocally expressed an intent to accept the offer, because it stated an intent to perform.

III. CLASS DISCUSSION

A. The Socratic Method

Relatively little legal instruction is presented in lecture form. Instead, law faculty will engage in more interactive teaching techniques, so that you can actively engage in the kind of analytic thinking and expression that lawyers must regularly perform. Teaching methods of this kind can take several forms, including writing exercises, small-group problem solving, and simulations in which you will apply lawyering skills to specific tasks, such as contract negotiations or arguments before a judge. By far the most common interactive teaching method, however, is the Socratic method.

In the Socratic method, your professor will invite you to express your analysis of a judicial decision or hypothetical case by asking you a series of questions about it. If it works well, the questions might lead you to new insights, helping you to make connections that you did not quite make when preparing the case. On the other hand, if you stray from the path chosen by the professor, he or she might use a new series of questions to lead you further down the path you have chosen, to demonstrate that your chosen path leads to an analytic dead end or to absurd results. By thus leading you in an exploration of the legal analysis, your teacher will attempt to illustrate patterns of analysis to the entire class.

Although the best professors do not use the Socratic method to embarrass or frustrate students, few students look forward to being put on the spot in this fashion. They typically fear the reactions of their peers more than the judgments of their professor. You can minimize this anxiety by coming to class well prepared so that you do not slow down the class discussion for lack of careful reading.

If you are prepared, your classmates will be understanding if you stumble a bit during the Socratic dialogue; after all, it will be their turn soon. Just take a deep breath, relax, think deeply about your professor's questions, answer them as best you can, and learn as much as you can from your professor's reactions to your responses.

During class, be prepared for questions that seem to have no certain answer. The answers to many legal questions will be something like, "It depends," meaning that the outcome will depend on further facts and on how a judge or jury will apply the law to the facts in a close case.

Indeed, you might be tempted to complain that your professor supplies more questions than answers during class. You might be right about your professor's actions, but that does not mean you have reason to complain. Your professor is helping you to identify the important questions, but the most interesting of those questions might have no certain answer. To maximize your learning in these conditions, you must gain comfort with uncertainty.

B. Gaining Comfort with Uncertainty

1. When the Answer Is Uncertain, Develop Arguments

Chapter 2 explained that, like a basketball game yet to be played, the most interesting legal questions have no certain answer, at least not until the highest court or other final legal authority on that issue declares its answer. Even then, the answer is "correct" only because the legal system gives finality to the decisions rendered by that authority; it is not the only plausible answer that the authority could have embraced. Moreover, the answer might enjoy its status as binding law only temporarily, until replaced by a different "answer" as the law evolves to meet the expanding knowledge and changing needs of society.

Consequently, when your textbook or your professor raises a novel legal question that has not yet been definitively resolved within the state or other relevant jurisdiction, it is not your responsibility as a law student or later as an attorney to reveal the "correct answer" to your professor or your client. Instead, you can describe the alternative outcomes, identify the legal and factual arguments that support each outcome, and make a prediction about which outcome you believe is most strongly supported by the law and the facts. If you can recognize this inherent uncertainty in the law, and if you can appreciate that many of the questions raised in class by your professor have no certain answers, you will find your study of the law to be much more rewarding and less frustrating, and you will perform much better on most law school essay exams.

Your primary tasks on such questions are to recognize the precise question that is presented, to compare the merits of any competing legal rules that might apply to resolve the question, and to analyze whether the facts satisfy the requirements of the selected legal rule, taking care to argue both sides of the dispute. You will be expected to make a prediction about the outcome of such a legal dispute, or to otherwise take a position on the question, but the conclusion you favor is the least important part of your analysis; after all, your professor probably carefully crafted the question so that he or she cannot be certain of the answer that a court would provide.

So, when your professors ask questions in class but do not supply answers, they are not trying to confuse you by playing "hide the ball" in the classroom; instead they are training you to appreciate both sides of a dispute and to develop reasonable arguments for both sides. When such occasions arise, free yourself from the tyranny of the need to find a single answer. Instead, learn as much as you can from the kinds of questions your professors ask and the kinds of arguments they solicit from students.

2. An Illustration in a Nonlegal Context

Many professors of legal method and writing use demonstrations with fruits and vegetables to introduce new law students to fundamental concepts of common law legal method, such as the process of drawing analogies or distinctions between a previous decision and a new case, in the face of legal uncertainty. I use a version of this problem that I call the *Grocer's Problem*, which I adapted from a simpler version created by another teacher:

> You are a new employee at a small grocery store facing a shaded pedestrian sidewalk in a downtown urban center. The owner or manager of the grocery store (the "grocer") instructs you to stock fresh produce in the appropriate place in the store as soon as it arrives from suppliers.
>
> You notice that fruits and vegetables are stocked in two different places in the store: some in a display case behind a window facing the sidewalk and some in bins or on shelves in the interior of the store. When you asked the grocer where produce should be stocked, the grocer supplied a general rule: "If the fruit or vegetable would tend to attract shoppers into the store— pedestrians who were not already planning to enter the store—it belongs in the window display case; otherwise, place it in the appropriate place in the interior of the store."

During your first morning on the job, two crates of fresh produce arrived from suppliers. The first was a crate of clean, shiny, large, round, red apples. The grocer regarded the apples for a moment and instructed you to put them in the window display case. An hour later, a crate of carrots arrived, fresh from the ground and still dusty with soil, and the grocer instructed you to put them in the appropriate place in the interior of the store.

At noon, the grocer left for lunch, reminding you to stock fresh produce as soon as it arrives. Within minutes, a crate of clean, shiny, large, red bell peppers arrived, slightly taller than wide, and with some vertical grooves or ribbing, but generally round in shape. Where should you display the red bell peppers?

Here's the most important point about the Grocer's Problem. If you asked me "What's the answer?" I would truthfully respond, "I don't know; I designed the problem so that it would have no certain answer." If you can accept that completely truthful response, you are on the right track.

Following is an analysis of the problem from a faculty perspective. It should provide you with insights into the kinds of analytic skills that many faculty seek to develop in their students.

In law school, you will be exposed to the concept of *legal realism,* a view of the U.S. legal system that took hold in the twentieth century. It argues that legal rules are flexible, that the effective meanings of legal rules are those announced by judges and other officials who implement the rules, and that the interpretation of law provided by those officials is partly a product of the officials' values and their desires to advance important social policies. In a rough analogy to this concept of legal realism, we might say that the answer to the question about the proper location of the produce is the location that would be selected by the grocer if the grocer were present. Because you are eager to please your boss, your inquiry amounts to predicting how the grocer would assess the qualities of the red bell peppers, just as a lawyer might try to predict how the state supreme court would rule on a novel question of state law.

We have some basis for predicting the location that the grocer would choose. The grocer is apparently motivated by a desire to maximize the number of customers and sales that are produced by the contents of the window display case. To advance that policy, the grocer stated a general rule governing such matters: Place produce in the interior of the store unless it would tend to attract pedestrians into the store if placed in the window display case. Beyond that general rule, the grocer has issued two decisions in previous cases. The previous decisions, which we will call "precedent," held that the apples should be placed in the window display case and that the carrots should be placed in the interior of the store. We can imagine that the grocer's stated rule is like a statute or is like a common law rule established by the state's highest court. The grocer's decisions about the apples and the carrots are like two judicial opinions interpreting the statute, or providing further definition to the common law rule.

We should assume that the grocer, like U.S. courts, will follow the grocer's own precedent absent a very good reason for a change in course, so we can predict that the grocer will apply the general rule in a similar fashion in the future. For example, if a crate of clean, shiny, large, round, red apples arrives next week, we have a good basis for predicting that the grocer will direct employees to place those apples in the window display case.

The new case, however, does not present a question about apples; the new case raises a question about the location of red bell peppers, an issue that no previous decision of the grocer has addressed. A little thought will show that, even armed with the grocer's general rule and two previous decisions, you cannot predict with certainty where the grocer would place the red bell peppers. You can safely assume that the grocer would place the peppers in the window display case if the grocer would conclude that the peppers shared the apples' tendency to attract pedestrians into the store. However, we could best make that determination if we knew the grocer's rationale for the previous two decisions, if we knew the reasoning on which the grocer concluded that the apples, but not the carrots, would satisfy the grocer's rule by tending to attract pedestrians into the store.

If the grocer had provided a rationale for the previous decisions, we could then apply that rationale to the new case of the peppers. But, like some judicial opinions that are not as clearly or completely explained as we might like, the grocer's decisions did not express the grocer's rationale for concluding that the grocer's rule was satisfied in one case but not the other. That omission leaves us free to offer our own theories about the rationale behind the grocer's decisions, providing us with some creative room for argument.

Ask yourself why the grocer might have concluded in the two previous decisions that the apples would attract pedestrians but the carrots would not. Can you think of more than one theory that explains the two previous cases? Once you have identified a theory or rationale that explains the application of the grocer's rule in each of the two previous cases, apply that rationale to the case of the red peppers to make a prediction about where the grocer would place the peppers. If you were able to identify more than one theory or rationale that consistently explains each of the two previous cases, do the competing theories dictate a single conclusion for the red bell peppers?

When I lead this exercise for students or fellow faculty, I hear many possible explanations for the previous two decisions, and nearly all of them are reasonable and plausible. I mention here two competing explanations that are quite plausible and that serve to illustrate my point about uncertainty in the outcomes of legal disputes.

Some participants will argue that the grocer must have reasoned that the pleasing appearance of the apples would tend to attract shoppers into the store. Thus, a pedestrian passing by, although not previously intending to enter the store, might have his or her eyes drawn to the vibrant red color and pleasingly round shape of the large apples, and—in pausing—might then remember a few items on the grocery list that should be purchased without delay.

This rationale for the case of the apples also helps explain the case of the carrots: The dull, dusty, unwashed carrots would not likely attract customers into the store based on their visual appearance. Accordingly, the grocer placed the carrots in the interior of the store, accessible to those who planned to shop for carrots.

Applying this rationale to the red bell peppers, one might reasonably predict that the grocer would place the peppers in the window display case, because the peppers share many of the visually appealing characteristics of the apples: They are shiny, red, large, and generally round in shape. Of course, the peppers are different in appearance from the apples in some respects, so the analogy between the apples and the peppers is imperfect, and participants in the exercise might reach different conclusions when applying this rationale to the case of the bell peppers. Most of them, however, find that the peppers share the visual appeal of the apples to a sufficient degree to satisfy the grocer's rule for placing produce in the window display case.

Some students, however, inevitably offer an entirely different rationale for the grocer's conclusion that the apples would attract pedestrians to enter the store: The apples are ready to eat and thus would be a convenient snack for a hungry person passing by the store. Under that reasoning, a pedestrian who had not planned to enter the store might notice the apples, might realize that he or she could purchase an apple and immediately eat it on the way home, and then—on entering the store to do so—might remember other items that should be purchased. One fellow faculty member referred to this theory as the "snackability" rationale. This rationale also helps to explain the placement of the carrots in the interior of the store, because unwashed, unpeeled, dusty carrots would not appeal to a hungry pedestrian as a ready-to-eat snack and thus would best be stocked in the interior of the store, waiting to be purchased by a shopper who arrived on a planned shopping trip with a list of things to buy.

When applied to the red bell peppers, the "snackability" rationale would strongly support an argument that the peppers would be placed in the interior of the store, along with the carrots, contrary to the conclusion that would be strongly supported by a rationale based on visual appeal. Even though the peppers are clean, they are still more like the carrots than the apples with respect to their appeal as an immediate snack "on the go." Many shoppers might plan to cook bell peppers or serve them raw in slices in a salad, but very few people passing by on the sidewalk would run into a store to buy a red bell pepper on impulse, to munch on like an apple on the way home. True, even under this rationale, a student might plausibly argue to the contrary, based on an optimistic view about the grocer's assessment of the "snackability" of a red bell pepper. Nonetheless, most students applying this rationale would place the red bell peppers in the interior of the store.

Other theories might also reasonably explain the previous two cases and provide a basis for predicting the outcome of the new case. The two just presented, however, suffice to illustrate my point. Even with the guidance provided by a general rule and two previous cases applying the rule, advocates can reasonably argue for two different conclusions in the new case of the red bell peppers. If one advocate represented a client who wanted the bell peppers placed in the window display case, and another advocate represented a client who wanted the bell peppers placed in the interior of the store, the advocates would try to persuade the grocer (or the grocer's employee) that the previous decisions should be interpreted to support one conclusion or the other in the new case. Until the grocer reveals his or her reasoning more clearly and decides the new case, no one can say that the question posed in the new case has a certain answer.

Similarly, many of the questions posed by your professors, both in class and on exams, will have no certain answers. You should accept that point and embrace the task of developing arguments for either side or both sides of the dispute. Even when you are studying a judicial opinion in a decided case, when the outcome of that particular case is no longer uncertain, you can still appreciate that the case might have presented a close question that could have been reasonably resolved in other ways. Thus, you should not be afraid to read such cases with a critical eye, ready to defend a dissenting opinion or to develop your own argument that the case was decided wrongly.

III. THE NEXT STEP

Once you have critically analyzed and briefed a series of cases, and are prepared for class discussion, you must take a series of steps in preparing for examinations. From the first day of class, you should develop a strategy for taking notes when others are speaking in class, and for reviewing and refining your notes after class. During the process of reviewing past notes and preparing for the next class, one of the most meaningful tasks you can undertake is to refine your syntheses of cases that address the same topic, a process that will later facilitate your outlining of course material. For much more on note taking, review of notes, and the process of synthesis, turn to Chapter 5.

PART THREE

PREPARING FOR EXAMS

If you have adopted the advice offered in Part II of this book, you are diligently preparing thorough case briefs for each class and are willing to embrace the uncertainty that is inherent in legal analysis. To be fully prepared for exams, however, you must supplement your class preparation and participation with periodic activities through which you review course material and work with it in new ways. Specifically, you should:

■ take, review, and refine class notes, with special attention to case synthesis;

■ outline course material; and

■ research the types of exams that your professors are likely to give.

CHAPTER 5

Reviewing Class Notes and Synthesizing Cases

For most students, creating a course outline is the most important step in preparing for exams. Outlining can be extremely difficult, however, unless you have paved the way every day by taking helpful notes in class and by reviewing and refining those notes soon afterward. As you do so, you should take care to ensure that you have synthesized cases that address the same topic, because your case synthesis will provide an important foundation for your outlining.

I. TAKING AND REVIEWING CLASS NOTES

A. Staying Engaged During Class

Every time you enter the classroom, adopt the goal of taking meaningful notes that will lighten your load when you later review for exams. If you take this goal to heart, you might find the motivation to stay alert in class, constantly looking for opportunities to make mental connections with the course material. Every moment in which you are fully engaged in class can translate to greater efficiency in reviewing the course material in the hectic days and weeks prior to exams.

Meaningful class notes are not verbatim transcriptions of classroom dialogue. If you take down every spoken word on your laptop computer, you will leave yourself no time to think during class and will end up with voluminous notes that are too heavy to digest.

The best notes are ones that supplement your case briefs with new ideas and connections that come to mind as you are listening intently and mentally working with the material. Accordingly, you should spend most of your time during class engaged in the activity of *thinking*, ready to record helpful observations, conclusions, or even newly significant questions, as they occur to you. When you later review such notes, you will find that they yield helpful reminders of significant points, like an orchard of well-spaced fruit trees, rather than a forest so thick with underbrush that you can barely make out the trees.

B. Reviewing and Refining Your Notes

Every professor has noticed that conscientious students engage in a useful activity immediately after class if they have no immediate appointment elsewhere. The students *stay in their seats* at the end of class and clean up their notes (or they find a seat nearby if another class must immediately use the same classroom). They notice gaps where the ideas came too quickly for good note-taking, and they fill in those gaps while the discussion is still fresh in their minds. They note areas of confusion and they either puzzle it through or they approach the professor with questions before the professor packs up and leaves the room. They use their notes from class discussion to correct errors that they now see in their case briefs, and they strike out notes that seemed helpful when they were recorded but on later reflection appear to be insignificant and distracting.

If you make such an effort as soon as possible after class, your outlining and other exam-review activities will come much more easily. When you thus review and refine your notes, you should pay special attention to your synthesis of cases, an element of your analysis that is sufficiently important to warrant substantial discussion.

II. CASE SYNTHESIS

By learning to synthesize legal authorities, such as by comparing the facts and outcomes of two or more judicial decisions that address the same general legal issue, you can prepare for exams in three ways. First, you will have a deeper understanding of the law if you carefully analyze and synthesize cases than if you simply read some abstract statement of the law. Second, the process of synthesis helps you develop analytic skills that you will apply on an examination, because it can help you evaluate the merits of competing legal rules or understand how changes in facts might affect arguments and outcomes under the same legal rule. Third, synthesis of cases can be an effective bridge to outlining course material, which is perhaps the most important tool for reviewing a course and preparing for the final exam. In light of the importance of the process of case synthesis, you should synthesize related cases as you brief the cases before class, and you should later refine your case synthesis when you review your notes after class.

A. Backing Up to See the Whole Forest (and Not Just Individual Trees)

As previously noted, a judicial decision setting forth a court's resolution of a legal dispute is commonly called a *case*. When you study a case in isolation, you will strive—among other things—to understand the issue or issues presented to the court for resolution, the court's answer to the question raised by each of the issues, and the court's reasoning in reaching each of its conclusions. In explaining its reasoning, the court might review the law as it has developed up to that point. As it does so, it might synthesize previous cases by comparing the facts, holdings, and reasoning of these previous judicial decisions.

The court engages in this process of *synthesizing* cases because it recognizes that a case read in isolation is only one piece of a much larger puzzle. To see the broader contours of an area of the law, one must see how the current case fits together with other cases that have addressed the same general issue on a variety of facts. When the court compares the outcomes of previous cases on different facts, it can gain a better appreciation of the content of the applicable legal rules and how the rules have applied to various facts.

The court can then reach its conclusion in the case currently before it— its "holding"—by applying its understanding of the legal rule to the facts of the current case. As it does so, it might continue to draw guidance from the previous cases by determining the extent to which the facts of the current dispute are analogous to, or distinguishable from, those of previous cases whose outcomes are known.

You will engage in a similar process when briefing cases, as a bridge to outlining course material. When you study two or more cases that address generally the same legal issue, albeit on different facts, you should go beyond analyzing each case in isolation. In the synthesis section of your briefs of the second and succeeding cases, you should also summarize the way in which that case's treatment of the issue compares with the treatment of the same issue in other cases.

For example, does the case you are currently briefing reach a different holding on the same general issue than did a previous case you studied earlier in the week? If yes, and if the courts applied the same legal rule in both cases, can you identify differences in the facts of the cases that justify different outcomes? If so, you have a classic synthesis at hand: two cases addressing the same issue and applying the same legal rule to different facts, but reaching opposite conclusions because the factual differences placed the cases on opposite sides of the line between satisfying and failing to satisfy the legal rule.

Of course, other results are possible from a synthesis of two or more cases. Several cases, for example, might reach the same conclusion after applying the same legal rule to a variety of different facts, thus providing a broader picture of the full range of facts that courts have found to satisfy the rule (or fail to satisfy it, if that is the outcome in all the cases). Or the case that you are currently briefing might adopt a different legal rule from that applied in two other cases that you have recently briefed, perhaps because it was decided in a different era or in a different state. Furthermore, some disputes might require a synthesis of several different kinds of legal authority, such as statutory text, judicial decisions that interpret that text, and constitutional provisions that invalidate a portion of the statute or its application.

The possibilities are numerous, but making these comparisons and distinctions explicit will help you to move beyond a laundry list of unrelated case briefs to a fuller understanding of the law reflected in the cases. The metaphor of being able to see the shape of the forest as a whole, rather than getting lost in an undifferentiated mass of shrubs and trees, is particularly apt here.

B. Taking Your Legal Writing Course Seriously

Your legal writing course likely will provide you with explicit training in synthesizing cases and other legal authorities, perhaps in the context of your preparing office memoranda and court briefs. As painful as it might be to receive critical feedback early in your studies, do not miss the chance to learn from every editorial comment from your legal writing professor. If your other professors are not giving you equally critical feedback, it is probably because they are content to evaluate your performance on the basis of a single final exam at the end of the course, after it is too late for you to learn from the exam and affect your grade. In comparison, the constructive criticism that you receive throughout the semester in your legal writing course should be treated as a precious (even if sometimes painful) gift.

Working diligently on office memoranda for your legal writing class is helpful to your exam preparation in a more general way. The "Discussion" section of an office memorandum typically follows the pattern of deductive reasoning that you will apply on an essay exam: For every issue that you identify, you need to summarize the legal rule or rules that help resolve that issue, apply the rule or rules to the facts, and reach a reasonable conclusion. Thus, many of the assignments in your legal writing course will help you develop skills of analysis, organization, and expression that will help you do your best on essay examinations.

C. Examples of Case Synthesis

The insights that might emerge from synthesizing cases come in so many different forms that the best way to learn is through illustrations and exercises. Following are two illustrations, the first set in a nonlegal context and the second in a legal context.

1. Warm-Up: Example in a Nonlegal Context

For a simple nonlegal example, imagine that you are in high school again, and your parents are reacting to your evening social activities. You know from experience that your parents are concerned about your health and safety, including your getting enough sleep, and about your reserving sufficient time for homework each week. Still, they have not advanced these policy concerns by announcing a general restriction on your activities, as a legislature might do when it enacts a statute.

Instead, they simply react to your extracurricular activities on a case-by-case basis. With each reaction, they decide whether a particular activity was appropriate or inappropriate, and they do their best to explain their reasons for the decision. In so doing, your parents are acting like a common law court, reaching decisions in particular cases and thus developing their rules incrementally. Their holding in each case combines with previous holdings to form a fuller view of the rules. With these assumptions, read, interpret, and synthesize the following four cases.

> **Case 1:** On Friday night, you attended the high school football game with a friend, catching a ride with your friend's older brother. After the game, the three of you joined other friends at B's Pizza Parlor, eating pizza and then hanging out for nearly an hour to socialize after finishing the pizza. Your friend and his brother brought you back home shortly after 11:00 P.M. Your parents are clearly unhappy, asking you where you had gone after the game, pointing to their watches, and—on learning that you had gone to the pizza parlor—admonishing you for going there after the football game. They decide to ground you from extracurricular activities for the remainder of the weekend.

The only "law" known to you at this point is your parents' reaction to this single event. Their disposition is clear: They have concluded that you violated some rule that might have been only implicit before this night but is now taking more concrete form as a consequence of this evening's activities. Because you want to avoid being grounded in the future, you are anxious to derive some sort of lesson from this case, so that you can apply it to future cases. As a first step, you want to understand your parents' "holding" in the case, which you might define as their disposition or resolution in light of facts that they deemed to be important. If you can accurately define this holding, if you compare the critical facts of this case to those of a future case, and if your parents strive for consistency in their actions, then you might have a basis for predicting their reaction in the future case.

You can readily see, however, that the holding of the current case is a matter of interpretation. Were your parents displeased because you came home at too late an hour, or because you went to a pizza parlor that they deemed to be unsafe at night, or simply because you did not inform them of your postgame activities, or a combination of these factors? A number of interpretations are reasonable, and this uncertainty about the precise holding of Case 1 creates uncertainty about the content of the rule that your parents are developing.

Case 1 thus leaves room for argument about how the rule of this case might apply to a future case. Interestingly, you might gain some insights about the holding of the first case, and about the rule that is taking shape in the first case, by seeing another case and synthesizing it with the first one.

Case 2: The next Friday night, you once again attended the football game, and once again ate pizza afterward at B's Pizza Parlor with your friend and his older brother. This time, however, you called your parents by cell phone after the game and informed them that you were going to B's Pizza Parlor after the game. They told you to have a good time, which you did by eating plenty of pizza and socializing with friends after the last piece was consumed. Although you once again arrived home slightly after 11 P.M., your parents welcomed you home without any admonishments.

By comparing and contrasting Case 2 with Case 1, you might be able to isolate the factor or factors that your parents deem to be critical in each case. Your parents reached different conclusions in the cases, but your activities each week were identical except for one fact: In Case 2, you informed your parents of your postgame plans. Thus, by synthesizing the cases, you can derive a more accurate sense of the holding of each case, and you can begin to formulate a rule that explains both cases. Specifically, you have discovered that returning home shortly after 11 P.M. is not a problem on a Friday night and that B's Pizza Parlor is not forbidden territory, but that you must inform your parents if you go someplace after the game before returning home.

Case 3: On the next Friday night, your actions were identical to those in Case 2, except that you socialized at the pizza parlor until it closed at midnight, returning home about ten minutes after midnight. Your parents grounded you for a week.

If you synthesize all three of these cases, you see a new factor emerging. You informed your parents of your postgame plans this week, yet they still disapproved of your actions. The only factor that changed between the second and third week was the time you returned home. Although you cannot know for certain at what moment you violated your parents' unstated curfew, you can infer that your returning home after midnight exceeded the limits of their patience.

Case 4: When your family attended your cousin's wedding on a Saturday night, you found yourself staying up late with them at the reception. Although you and your younger brother complained about being bored after 10 P.M., your parents danced to every number that the band played until the band stopped at 11 P.M. and, afterward, your parents continued to laugh and talk with friends and relatives until past 11:30 P.M. By the time your family returned home, it was past midnight. You complained about being stuck so long at the reception, because you needed to get up early for church the next day. Your parents sympathized, but they explained the importance of the event to the extended family, and they thanked you for staying up late with them.

At first glance, your parents' behavior in Case 4 seems so contrary to their reactions in Case 3 that you might accuse them of making decisions based on transitory self-interest or whim. If that is your first reaction, you can identify with students of the law who believe that some judicial decisions are dictated by the social or political biases of the judges rather than by a consistent and principled application of rules. This cynicism is justifiable to some degree; after all, any judge inevitably brings to the bench a personal perspective and a set of values based on a lifetime of personal experiences, and those perspectives and values are bound to influence how a judge interprets rules and applies them to facts. Moreover, courts in different states are free to adopt different rules of state common law, just as different families are free to adopt different family rules. Nonetheless, before concluding that a line of decisions is internally inconsistent, do your best to synthesize the cases and attempt to construct a rule that explains all of them in some principled manner, particularly if all the cases are issued by the same court.

For example, in Case 4, your parents might explain that the very valid interests in providing you with ample time for homework and sleep must occasionally give way to the greater interest in fully attending an important family event, such as the wedding of a close relative. Moreover, because the whole family participates in such an event, your parents are able to view and supervise your activities, thus eliminating uncertainty about your movements and about the risks that you might be taking.

If you synthesize all four of the cases, you should be able to derive a reasonable statement of the rules and exception that your parents have developed, incrementally, on a case-by-case basis:

You must inform your parents of plans to extend your social activities beyond the initial outing for which they gave permission, and you must return home by midnight, even on a weekend, unless you are attending an important family event that keeps you out later.

This statement is not the only reasonable product of your synthesis of the cases; other formulations are possible, because the cases are reasonably subject to different interpretations. Moreover, this statement of your parents' rule is not necessarily complete; other facets of their rules could emerge in future cases. Nonetheless, this is one reasonable statement of the set of rules that you could derive from these four cases.

2. Example in a Legal Context

The following example provides a second illustration of synthesis, this one set in the legal field of remedies and raising issues about permissible awards of money damages for breach of contract. The illustration begins with a brief summary of fundamental legal principles; however, you will derive your understanding of the rule in question primarily by reading summaries of cases that resolve specific disputes on different facts. If the holding of each case is a piece in a jigsaw puzzle, your synthesis of the cases should produce a fuller picture of the completed puzzle.

Let's start with some basic law of damages to set the background. An award of compensatory damages is a sum of money designed to compensate a party for the actual injury or losses sustained by that party. Punitive damages are an additional sum of money designed to punish a wrongdoer for an egregious breach of duty, and to deter others from such misconduct by making an example of the wrongdoer.

Damages of some type might be awarded for breach of a contract, which arises out of a voluntary agreement between two or more parties, or for a tort, which consists of the breach of a duty that arises out of community standards of care and decency owed to others.

Suppose we studied a number of judicial decisions, or "cases," from the appellate courts of a state on this topic, and we derived the following holdings from those cases:

A v. B (1991): When an employer fired an employee in violation of a contract clause requiring good cause for termination of the contract, the jury properly awarded compensatory damages, but it was not authorized to award punitive damages for the employer's intentional breach of an employment contract.

C v. D (2005): The jury properly awarded compensatory damages, but it was not authorized to award punitive damages for a contractor's inadvertent breach of contract when it excavated an area for a parking garage 20 feet further north than called for by the contract.

***E v. F* (1967):** The jury properly awarded compensatory damages, but it was not authorized to award punitive damages for a well owner's breach of contract to supply water to a neighbor, even though the well owner acted maliciously to injure the neighbor by shutting off the water supply.

***G v. H* (1896):** The jury properly awarded both compensatory and punitive damages against a man who breached his promise to marry his fiancée, leaving her humiliated and devalued in the eyes of her peers.

***I v. J* (1974):** The jury properly awarded compensatory damages, but it was not authorized to award punitive damages for a manufacturer's breach of its contract to sell factory machinery to a factory owner, even though the manufacturer breached intentionally to take advantage of market prices that had risen since it had entered into the contract.

***K v. L* (1989):** The jury properly awarded both compensatory and punitive damages against an employer who subjected an employee to such egregious sexual harassment that the employer committed the tort of intentionally inflicting emotional distress on the employee. The employer also breached the employment contract, but that provided no basis for the punitive damage award.

The cases are presented here in seemingly random fashion, as you might encounter them in the library when conducting research. If you organize and synthesize them, however, you can see a pattern emerging: With one exception, the courts in this state are consistent in withholding punitive damages for breach of contract in a wide variety of contexts, including employment, construction, the supply of water, and the sale of machinery. Moreover, the courts adhere to that position even in the case of intentional breaches, and even if the breach is maliciously intended to harm the other party. The courts of this state did, however, permit punitive damages in a case in which the breach of contract was accompanied by an intentional tort. Thus, a synthesis of all the cases other than *G v. H* could produce the following plausible rule: A jury is authorized to award punitive damages for an egregious tort, but not solely for breach of contract, even if the breach is intentional or even malicious.

The case of *G v. H*, however, is more difficult to reconcile with the other cases, because it apparently authorizes punitive damages for a breach of contract without a separate finding of a tort. This apparent aberration adds some uncertainty to the law that has emerged from your synthesis of the cases. Perhaps the unique character of an agreement to marry, and the kinds of emotional injury that are likely to result from its breach, justify an exception to the general rule. Alternatively, you might conclude that this nineteenth-century decision reflects outdated and sexist notions about the significance of a broken engagement, and you might predict that its holding would be rejected by the state's appellate courts if the same issue arose today.

Regardless of how you analyze and synthesize these cases, you can see that studying and comparing a number of cases might enable you to derive general rules that you can apply to future cases presenting new facts. You cannot expect your synthesis of every line of cases to be perfectly smooth; you should instead expect some rough edges and ambiguity. You should strive to work comfortably with those rough edges; after all, there would be little work for you and your classmates after graduation if the law and its application to new facts were perfectly certain, without room for argument. Your bread and butter as an attorney will be the arguments you can make on behalf of a client in the face of uncertainty in the law. In law school, if you can quickly develop a facility for recognizing uncertainty in a legal rule or in its application to facts, and if you can argue both sides of such disputes, you will be better prepared both for your exams and for the practice of law.

III. THE NEXT STEP

Let's suppose that the semester has progressed and that you are becoming adept at analyzing and synthesizing cases. Further, you have reached the end of a unit of study in one of your courses, providing you with an opportunity to review that subject area. At this point, you should organize your thoughts in a form that will facilitate your review of the course material for a midterm or final exam. The perfect vehicle for this is a course outline, described in detail in the next chapter.

CHAPTER 6

Outlining Course Material

Commercial outlines of various courses are available in bookstores, and they might be useful to you as one of several types of resources to which you refer occasionally to help clear up confusion about the law you are studying. Each professor, however, has different views about helpful terminology, coverage of issues, points of emphasis, and important themes underlying the course. Accordingly, no generic study guide can be tailored to the particular course that your professor offers.

Moreover, any text is a just a collection of words, and those words will be meaningful to you only to the extent that you have worked with the legal material in ways that develop your skills of analysis and expression. In turn, your exams will require application of those skills and a working knowledge of the law, not just a regurgitation of words that spell out a rule.

For most students, the best way to develop these skills and a working knowledge of the law is to develop their own outlines of each course, either working independently or in small study groups. Such an outline, tailored to your course and your professor's views about the course, will be an excellent study guide and will help you see how the elements of your course fit together in the "big picture." If you like graphics, you may wish to supplement your outlines with flowcharts that highlight issues and decision points in an analysis.

Moreover, the process of creating the outline will develop the skills and working knowledge that you seek to acquire. Indeed, after completing the outline, if you suffered the misfortune of losing your only copy of it, you would still be better off than if you had spent money on a commercial outline, because your level of understanding of the material would be vastly increased by the substantial intellectual labors that you invested in producing the outline.

I. WHY OUTLINE?

You will gain several benefits from producing outlines of complicated masses of material. First, to the extent that it allows you to summarize voluminous notes and other course materials, you can reduce your exam review guide to a manageable size. Second, a good outline requires you to engage in the analytic processes of categorizing and reorganizing materials, drawing connections between them, deriving rules from them, and recognizing how the contrasting facts of particular cases illustrate the satisfaction or nonsatisfaction of a rule. Engaging in these analytic activities will help you develop skills and acquire knowledge that you will later apply directly to essay exams, office memoranda, and briefs to a court.

Finally, you might think that you know the law that you are studying, but it is one thing to be comfortable with a fuzzy ball of concepts in your mind and entirely another thing to organize the legal concepts in a logical fashion and express the rules in your own words, reflecting a deep understanding. You will find that the task of outlining your course materials will reveal gaps in your knowledge, spurring you to fill the gaps and clear up the confusion while you outline, weeks before the exam. That is a much better state of affairs than recognizing your confusion only when you try to express your ideas on the exam itself.

II. THE OUTLINING PROCESS: GETTING STARTED

At the most general level, outlining requires you to categorize so that you can place information within a logically organized framework. If summarization was your only aim, you could simply set out your case briefs, one after another, and then try to condense them further while incorporating insights that you gleaned from class discussion. Your exam, however, will require you not merely to recall the holdings and reasoning of cases in your casebook, but also to spot issues and to apply your understanding of the law to the facts of new hypothetical cases that you have never seen before. To accomplish those tasks well, you must understand how the pieces of the law fit together, and how some rules and issues form subsets of more general principles and broader inquiries.

A. A Nonlegal Example

For example, imagine that you are a clerk in a grocery store and are helping move stock to new locations during a store remodeling. During that move, the existing stocks of candies were mixed together in a disorganized pile.

True, just like each of your case briefs, each item of candy is neatly packaged. However, your customers will be confused and frustrated if you simply place the items on the shelf randomly, in the order in which you happen to reach for each one in the box. So, what would you do?

You probably would begin by sorting the candy into general categories, so that those customers who want pure chocolate products can find them in one section of a shelf and can compare brands and cocoa content, while those hunting for licorice twists can compare brands, sizes, and prices of that product on a separate shelf. Thus, you are looking for ways in which some items share important characteristics that make them belong together within some more general classification.

After you sorted the candy into categories that would be helpful to shoppers, you would then place items that are not identical, but are in the same category, in some logical order in the same section of a shelf.

The following represents such a categorization in outline form, with much of the content omitted to give you a broad view of the structure:

Aisle 15A Products
I. Gum and Breath Mints
. . .
II. Candies
   A. Chocolate Bars and Related Products
      1. Premium Chocolates
         a. Chocolate Truffle Assortments
         . . .
         b. Premium Chocolate Bars
            (1) Premium Dark Chocolate Bars
               (a) Belgian and German Semi-Sweet
               (b) Latin-American Single-Origin
               . . .
            (2) Premium Bars with Milk Chocolate
            . . .
   B. Popular Candies with Chocolate
   . . .
   C. Fructose-Based Chewy Candies
   . . .

This list could go on for many pages, and in much more detail, as will your course outlines. Classification of cases and concepts in your course outline, however, will be a much more intellectually challenging exercise, because the concepts will likely be much less familiar to you than types of candy. Thus, an example in a legal setting will prove helpful.

B. Example: Misrepresentation and Nondisclosure in Contract Formation

In your Contracts course, you will learn that a contract is not enforceable against you if you were induced to enter into the contract by the other party's misrepresentation. Of course, whether you can avoid enforcement on that ground depends on a number of factors that help define the details of the rules governing this topic. To acquire a working knowledge of those rules, you will undoubtedly read background information in your casebook, analyze and synthesize cases, and draw further insights from class discussion.

After you complete your study of this unit in your Contracts course, let's suppose that you decide to add this topic to your running outline of that course. Even the few cases in that short unit introduced new terminology and several new concepts, and you might find yourself staring at four or five cases in your casebook, several pages of case briefs that you prepared for class, and handwritten notes or a computer file of notes from class discussion.

The table of contents of your casebook, or the assignments in your class syllabus, might help you see how this unit of study relates to other general topics of the course. When outlining this particular unit, however, you will need to develop some ideas for organizing your outline at a finer level of detail.

If you focused intently on the discussion during class, and if you reviewed your notes after each class, you might have already worked out in your mind how you intend to organize the material on misrepresentation in contract formation. If not, and if you have trouble getting started, you might want to identify all of the terms or concepts that the courts deemed to be important to their analyses and decisions, and then set them out randomly in a laundry list. If you took a few minutes to scan your notes and perhaps some terms that you underlined in your casebook, you would end up with a list similar to this:

> misrepresentation; half-truth; reliance; fact v. opinion; nondisclosure; material facts; falsehood; summary judgment; confidential or fiduciary relationship; justifiable; sales of homes; sales puffing; rescission; arm's length transaction

In making such a list, you should be fairly uninhibited; you are doing no more than focusing attention on some key terms as a way of starting some brainstorming.

As your next step, you should draw connections between terms that address similar topics, distinguish terms that address different topics, and determine which terms define general categories that encompass other concepts conveyed by other terms. After seeing the terms *misrepresentation* and *contract formation* in your list, for example, you recall the nature of this topic at its most general level. You quickly glance at the table of contents in your casebook, and you recall that this unit deals with one of several defenses to contract enforcement that could preclude enforcement of a contract. Accordingly, you could begin this section of your outline with a general heading that describes this unit and helps to show its place among other topics in your outline:

VII. Defenses to Enforcement
    A. Statute of Frauds: Absence of a Required Writing
      . . .
    B. Lack of Capacity
      . . .
    C. Duress
      . . .
    D. Misrepresentation During Contract Formation

Next, you remember from other units of study that *rescission* is an equitable remedy through which a court can cancel a contract that is unenforceable, and you also remember that the equitable nature of this remedy allows courts some flexibility in analyzing the elements of this defense, a point worth discussing in your outline. You also recall that the term *misrepresentation* not only was a popular way to refer to the defense as a whole, but was also used more specifically to refer to one of several elements of this defense to enforcement. As you recall those elements, you remember that the misrepresentation must be *material,* or important, to contract formation; otherwise, it would be harmless and would not warrant upsetting the contract. That thought, in turn, reminds you that—for the same reasons—the party seeking to deny enforcement must have relied on the misrepresentation in entering the contract or agreeing to particular terms.

So, what about the reference to "half-truth"? Maybe after glancing at your class notes or one of the cases in this unit, you recall from your reading and from class discussion that the term misrepresentation, as an element of the defense, was a general term that encompassed several different kinds of misrepresentation, including half-truth—or at least that's the terminology and categorization that your professor appeared to favor. Once down that path, you then look for other examples of specific forms of misrepresentation that belong with half-truth, and you recall that affirmative falsehoods, half-truths, and active concealment were all potentially forms of misrepresentation. So far, your skeletal outline of this unit might look like this:

> D. Misrepresentation During Contract Formation—A party can rescind a contract or otherwise avoid contract enforcement if it relied on a material misrepresentation in agreeing to the contract.
> 1. Misrepresentation—This can be in the form of a falsehood, half-truth, or active concealment of material information.
>   a. Falsehood—
>   b. Half-Truth—
>   c. Active Concealment—
> 2. Material—
> 3. Reliance—
> 4. Equity and Flexibility—

Do you see how the outline leads you to address topics first at the most general level and then in increasing detail? It is a little like viewing the broad contours of a forest from a distance of 100 yards, then walking closer to identify several species of trees that make up the forest, and then even closer to examine the characteristics of the bark, branches, and leaves of each species of tree. When you walk out of the forest again, you will see its broad outlines more clearly now, with a better understanding of how it fits into the geography of the surrounding area.

However, you have only scratched the surface. What about this term *justifiable* and the reference to fact versus opinion? After scanning your notes, you recall that each of these terms relates to others already in your outline. You recall, for example, that a party's reliance on a misrepresentation generally must be justifiable, rather than foolish. Moreover, you remember a general rule that parties are permitted some leeway in expressing *opinions*—sometimes in the form of "sales puffing" that extols the general virtues of a product or service—and you remember that only a misrepresentation of existing *fact* will warrant a defense to enforcement of a contract. You add to your outline accordingly:

> D. Misrepresentation During Contract Formation—A party can rescind a contract or otherwise avoid contract enforcement if it relied on a material misrepresentation in agreeing to the contract.
> > 1. Misrepresentation—This can be in the form of a falsehood, half-truth, or active concealment of material fact.
> > > a. Falsehood—
> > > b. Half-Truth—
> > > c. Active Concealment—
> > 2. Material—
> > 3. Fact, Rather Than Opinion—
> > 4. Reliance—
> > 5. Equity and Flexibility—

The only terms left in your brainstorming list are confidential or fiduciary relationship, summary judgment, sales of homes, and arm's length transaction. After a moment's reflection, you drop summary judgment from the list; it might have been important to your understanding of the procedural posture of a case, and your professor might have made some point about it in class discussion, but you realize that it relates to procedural rules that apply to any case and that it does not have special significance to this unit of study.

The significance of the remaining terms puzzles you at first, but a few minutes of reviewing your materials leads you to the conclusion that they are related to a subtopic, one that must have been challenging for you, because you left these terms for last. After rereading a case and some notes in your casebook, you put it together, at least at a general level: Simple nondisclosure of facts generally is not a ground for avoiding enforcement; however, this general rule is subject to exceptions in many states for sales of real estate or at least of dwellings, and in all states for transactions between parties with special relationships, such as confidential or fiduciary relationships. Some of these terms are still a little fuzzy to you, but you are beginning to recall readings and discussion about them, and you will cement your knowledge of them when forced to define them and provide examples of them in your outline. In the meantime, however, you decide to show how these remaining terms fit into the skeleton of your outline:

> D. Misrepresentation During Contract Formation—A party can rescind a contract or otherwise avoid contract enforcement if it relied on a material misrepresentation in agreeing to the contract.
> > 1. Misrepresentation—This can be in the form of a falsehood, half-truth, or active concealment of material fact.
> > > a. Falsehood—
> > > b. Half-Truth—
> > > c. Active Concealment—
> > > d. Nondisclosure—Nondisclosure generally is not a ground for avoidance, with common exceptions for special relationships and for sales of homes or possibly other real estate.
> > > > (1) Special Relationships—A confidential or fiduciary relationship might give rise to a duty to disclose material facts.
> > > > (2) Real Estate Transactions—By statute or by judicially created warranties, most states now follow a trend of requiring disclosure of material facts for sales of homes, and more broadly in some states for any sale of real estate.
> > 2. Material—
> > 3. Fact, Rather Than Opinion—
> > 4. Reliance—
> > 5. Equity and Flexibility—

III. PUTTING FLESH ON THE BONES OF YOUR OUTLINE

You can see now that your skeletal outline is a little like a tree, with the most general topic forming the trunk, major elements of this defense to enforcement forming the main branches, and subtopics and examples forming smaller branches and leaves. Your definitions of the general topic and of each element form rules, some of which divide further into subtopics and more specific definitions and rules.

Each time you struggle to categorize a concept and show its relationship to others, you are developing skills of issue spotting and organization. Each time you labor to express these definitions in your own words, you are practicing written expression so that the outlined material will flow more quickly and effortlessly during the exam. By taking the time to work through a definition in your outline, you are rooting it somewhere in your brain, like a body movement that is rooted in the muscle memory of a dancer or other athlete.

However, essay examinations also call for you to apply rules to facts, a form of analysis that requires more than memory of an array of rules. It requires an appreciation of the way in which facts arguably satisfy or fail to satisfy a rule, and the way in which different facts, or different ways of looking at the same fact, can support arguments for either conclusion about the satisfaction of a rule. Fortunately, because you have analyzed and synthesized many cases, you have seen and critiqued judicial reasoning in the application of rules to facts, and you have compared and contrasted cases to better understand how differing facts have influenced the outcomes in the cases. As you will soon see, your periodic synthesis of cases will form an effective bridge to your outlines.

You can summarize the insights that you glean from case analysis and synthesis by illustrating the satisfaction or nonsatisfaction of a rule with a brief summary of the holdings of cases that you briefed for class. Ideally, each summary will refer to critical facts or reasoning but will sum it up in a single sentence. For example, the following cases illustrate the breadth of the concept of half-truth, because both cases can be interpreted to find a misrepresentation by half-truth, although on very different facts:

> b. **_Half-Truth_**—A party engages in half-truth when he or she misleadingly addresses a topic by revealing some, but not all, of the material facts.
>
> (1) Example: In _Kannavos_ (CB at 357), advertisements created a false impression by revealing that property had been used as income-producing apartments, without revealing that this use violated zoning laws.
>
> (2) Example: In _Vokes_ (CB at 363), the court stated that dance instructors' flattery left a false impression when they failed to provide the "whole truth" about the student's limited potential.

Alternatively, if you synthesized two cases with _different_ outcomes on the same issue, and you found that differences in the facts justified the different outcomes, you are now armed with an excellent set of illustrations of the applicable rule: The differing facts and outcomes of the cases help to define the line between satisfaction and nonsatisfaction of the rule. For example, illustrations (a) and (b) in the following outline summarize interpretations of cases that reach different conclusions about a party's duty to disclose material facts, based on facts that establish the presence or absence of a special relationship:

> (1) Special relationships—A confidential or fiduciary relationship might give rise to a duty to disclose material facts.

(a) In *Swinton*, the seller was under no duty to disclose a hidden termite infestation, because the seller and buyer were strangers and thus were bargaining in an "arm's length" transaction rather than in the context of a special relationship.

(b) In contrast, under one interpretation of the *Vokes* case, the dance instructor had a fiduciary duty to disclose all material facts about the dancer's limited potential before signing her to lifetime contracts, because he was then performing a preexisting shorter term contract with her and thus was being paid to provide his expert advice and assessment.

(c) Note: Many states would now avoid enforcement on the facts of *Swinton*, because they would impose a duty to disclose material facts in the sale of a home, regardless of any special relationship between the parties.

When you thus illustrate the scope of a rule in your outline by comparing or contrasting the facts of different cases, you are developing skills of fact analysis applicable to an essay exam. You might not have time in your essay exam answer to explicitly compare or contrast the exam facts with the facts of a case summarized in your outline. However, your previous use of cases as illustrations of a rule will equip you to identify and develop factual arguments for your exam answer.

IV. USING YOUR OUTLINE AS A STUDY GUIDE

A. Learning Through Outlining

As should be clear by now, the process of constructing an outline might be your best form of exam preparation: It forces you to confront gaps in your knowledge and to work with your course material in a way that develops analysis, organization, and expression skills. If you never had the opportunity to read your outline after creating it, you would still be well prepared to take your exam. Ideally, of course, you would complete each outline a few days or a week before the exam, so that you could read your outline several times to help you remember the rules that you have derived from your studies and the way in which the facts of cases have satisfied or failed to satisfy those rules.

B. Spin-Offs from Your Main Outline

1. Outline of Main Headings

You can benefit further by adapting your outline to serve as a final study guide. For example, you can use your word processor to make an "outline of your outline." This shorter version will set forth the headings that identify major issues or topics, as well as major rules and definitions, allowing you to review the broad contours of your course. Although this shorter outline omits the fine details, by now you should be able to recall those details on any topic if the need arises.

2. Checklist of Issues
For still tighter focus, you should reduce your outline to a single page that sets forth a checklist of issues, adapted from the major section headings that identify general topics or issues. This very short version of your outline might not state any rules, but it will remind you of problem areas that could arise on the exam, helping you to identify issues to analyze.

3. Strategic Guide for Problem Solving
Finally, you might see the opportunity to adapt your materials in yet another way, at least for some courses. If the course you are studying lends itself to a particular mode of problem solving, you can generate a single-page strategic plan for addressing a problem. For example, in your Contracts course, you might decide that it will make sense for you first to determine whether a party might be able to bring a claim on an agreement (contract) or on some alternative basis for relief such as quasi-contract or promissory estoppel, or on two or more of these grounds. If so, you should make a checklist that starts with these issues:

> Basic Claims:
> Contract through agreement (look for this first)
> Quasi-contract, through unjust enrichment
> Promissory estoppel, through reliance on a promise

Next, if your exam question appears to raise a question about liability on a contractual agreement, you might then ask whether issues are raised at the stage of contract formation, performance, or enforcement (remedies), or some combination of these. Accordingly, the next three entries on your checklist might list these three stages. Next, you might address the possibility that the exam problem raises a question about contract formation, and you might select an order in which you will look for issues and analyze them if you find them raised by the facts of the problem. For example, you might decide that you prefer to first determine whether the facts raise a problem about reaching agreement through offer and acceptance, and then—assuming an agreement is arguably present—whether the facts raise a question about the traditional requirement of consideration.

Contract—look for issues at three stages in this order:
   Formation (including defects or misbehavior in formation)
   Performance (including interpretation questions)
   Remedies
   . . .
Contract formation:
   Offer & acceptance issues (first, because it's possible to agree to a
      transaction that lacks consideration)
   Consideration
   Defenses and defects (such as duress during bargaining, etc.)

You might not be familiar right now with all the terms presented in the previous paragraph, but the discussion should suffice to illustrate that your exam strategy checklist could lay out potential issues in a different order and organization than the way in which they appear in your case-book or your outline. The outline will present issues, topics, and rules in a logical order that effectively shows their relationships to one another. You might find, however, that a different mode of organizing a checklist of major issues conforms to your personal strategy about efficiently address-ing an exam question.

V. EXERCISES

A. Synthesizing Two Cases and Outlining Ads as Offers

Prepare case briefs of the following two cases. In your second case brief, include a section entitled "Synthesis," in which you contrast and compare their results and reasoning. Retailers' advertisements are now subject to various statutory and administrative regulations. However, for this exercise, let's return to the 1950s and assume that the only relevant law is the common law of contracts, specifically its rules on what constitutes an offer by a seller.

Craft v. Elder & Johnston Co.
38 N.E.2d 416 (Ohio Ct. App. 1941)

BARNES, Judge. . . .
   . . . On or about January 31, 1940, the defendant, the Elder & Johnston Company, carried an advertisement in the Dayton Shopping News, an offer for sale of a certain all electric sewing machine for the sum of $26 as a "Thursday Only Special." Plaintiff . . . alleges that the above publication is an advertising paper distributed in Montgomery County and throughout the city of Dayton; that on Thursday, February 1, 1940, she tendered to

the defendant company $26 in payment for one of the machines offered in the advertisement, but that defendant refused to fulfill the offer and has continued to so refuse. The petition further alleges that the value of the machine offered was $175 and she asks damages in the sum of $149 plus interest from February 1, 1940. . . .

The trial court dismissed plaintiff's petition as evidenced by a journal entry, the pertinent portion of which reads as follows: "Upon consideration the court finds that said advertisement was not an offer which could be accepted by plaintiff to form a contract, and this case is therefore dismissed with prejudice to a new action, at costs of plaintiff." . . .

We will now briefly make reference to some of the authorities. "It is clear that in the absence of special circumstances an ordinary newspaper advertisement is not an offer, but is an offer to negotiate—an offer to receive offers—or, as it is sometimes called, an offer to chaffer." Restatement of the Law of Contracts, Par. 25, Page 31. [Author's note: This refers to the Restatement (First) of Contracts, completed in 1932.]

Under the above paragraph the following illustration is given, "[A] clothing merchant, advertises overcoats of a certain kind for sale at $50. This is not an offer but an invitation to the public to come and purchase."

"Thus, if goods are advertised for sale at a certain price, it is not an offer and no contract is formed by the statement of an intending purchaser that he will take a specified quantity of the goods at that price. The construction is rather favored that such an advertisement is a mere invitation to enter into a bargain rather than an offer. So a published price list is not an offer to sell the goods listed at the published price." Williston on Contracts, Revised Edition, Vol. 1, Par. 27, Page 54.

"The commonest example of offers meant to open negotiations and to call forth offers in the technical sense are advertisements, circulars and trade letters sent out by business houses. While it is possible that the offers made by such means may be in such form as to become contracts, they are often merely expressions of a willingness to negotiate." Page on the Law of Contracts, 2d Ed., Vol. 1, Page 112, Par. 84. . . .

". . . [G]enerally a newspaper advertisement or circular couched in general language and proper to be sent to all persons interested in a particular trade or business, or a prospectus of a general and descriptive nature, will be construed as an invitation to make an offer." 17 Corpus Juris Secundum, Contracts, Page 389, § 46, Column 2. . . .

We are constrained to the view that the trial court committed no prejudicial error in dismissing plaintiff's petition.

The judgment of the trial court will be affirmed and costs adjudged against the plaintiff-appellant. Entry may be prepared in accordance with this opinion.

GEIGER, P. J., and HORNBECK, J., concur.

Lefkowitz v. Great Minneapolis Surplus Store
251 Minn. 188, 86 N.W.2d 689 (1957), Minn. S. Ct.

MURPHY, Justice

This is an appeal from an order of the Municipal Court of Minneapolis. . . . The order for judgment awarded the plaintiff the sum of $138.50 as damages for breach of contract.

This case grows out of the alleged refusal of the defendant to sell to the plaintiff a certain fur piece which it had offered for sale in a newspaper advertisement. It appears from the record that . . . the defendant published the following advertisement in a Minneapolis newspaper:

Saturday 9 A.M. . . .
1 Black Lapin Stole
Beautiful, worth $139.50. . . .
$1.00 First Come First Served

The record supports the findings of the court that on . . . the Saturday following the publication of the above-described ad[] the plaintiff was the first to present himself at the appropriate counter in the defendant's store and . . . demanded the . . . stole so advertised and indicated his readiness to pay the sale price of $1. . . . [T]he defendant refused to sell the merchandise to the plaintiff. . . .

The defendant relies principally on *Craft v. Elder & Johnston Co.* . . . On the facts before us we are concerned with whether the advertisement constituted an offer, and, if so, whether the plaintiff's conduct constituted an acceptance.

There are numerous authorities which hold that a particular advertisement in a newspaper or circular letter relating to a sale of articles may be construed by the court as constituting an offer, acceptance of which would complete a contract [citations omitted]. . . .

The authorities above cited emphasize that, where the offer is clear, definite, and explicit, and leaves nothing open for negotiation, it constitutes an offer, acceptance of which will complete the contract. The most recent case on the subject is *Johnson v. Capital City Ford Co.*, La. App., 85 So. 2d 75, in which the court pointed out that a newspaper advertisement relating to the purchase and sale of automobiles may constitute an offer, acceptance of which will consummate a contract and create an obligation in the offeror to perform according to the terms of the published offer.

Whether in any individual instance a newspaper advertisement is an offer rather than an invitation to make an offer depends on the legal intention of the parties and the surrounding circumstances. Annotation, 157 A.L.R. 744, 751; 77 C.J.S., Sales, § 25b; 17 C.J.S., Contracts, § 389. We are of the view on the facts before us that the offer by the defendant of the sale of the Lapin fur was clear, definite, and explicit, and left nothing open for negotiation.

The plaintiff having successfully managed to be the first one to appear at the seller's place of business to be served, as requested by the advertisement, and having offered the stated purchase price of the article, he was entitled to performance on the part of the defendant. . . .
Affirmed.

By now you've noticed that these cases reached different conclusions on whether the newspaper ad constituted an offer, to which the customer could bind the store by expressing acceptance. Let's also assume that your synthesis of the cases, when informed by class discussion, leads you to conclude that the two cases are legally consistent. In other words, let's assume that the law regarding offers in Ohio in 1941 is consistent with the law regarding offers in Minnesota in 1957. Accordingly, your briefing and synthesis of the two cases should reveal factual distinctions between the two cases, distinctions that explain why the ad in one case was an offer and the ad in the other case was not.

You will use the knowledge that you gleaned from your briefing and synthesis to fill out the details of the following outline of newspaper ads as offers. In outline section D below, you should try to state a general rule about newspaper ads as offers, one that explains both of the cases you briefed. Then, use a single sentence in each of the two examples to explain how critical facts of each case help to illustrate the rule by explaining why the facts satisfied the rule or did not do so. Italicized prompts will guide your efforts, and you can find a sample completed outline in Appendix A.

IV. Offer—An offer leads a reasonable person to understand that the offeror is committed to enter into a contract on definite terms and has empowered the offeree to create a contract by expressing agreement.
. . .
D. A seller's newspaper advertisement to sell goods at a certain price is reasonably interpreted . . . , unless . . . . [*Complete this sentence to state a single, general rule that explains both cases.*]
    1. Example: In *Craft*, . . . [*Complete this sentence with a statement of the way in which the critical facts of this case illustrate your statement of the rule in section D above and explain the result of the case.*]
    2. Example: In contrast, in *Lefkowitz*, . . . [*Complete this sentence with a statement of the way in which the facts of this case illustrate your statement of the rule in section D above and explain the result of the case.*]
    3. Comment: Because most newspaper advertisements are as general as that in *Craft*, some authorities state a general rule that newspaper advertisements are not offers absent "special circumstances."

B. Advanced Exercise: Outlining Consideration

After you have studied consideration in your Contracts course, think about how you would organize the basic concepts in an outline. The following skeleton outline is just one of many reasonable ways of characterizing and organizing the critical elements of the topic. Consider whether you would change anything about this basic outline of issues and topics in light of how your course presented the material. Then, fill in the details of the outline, as prompted by the italicized instructions, and in the manner recommended in the preceding section. You can compare your outline with the sample for this exercise in Appendix A.

I. Consideration—[*State a definition at the most general level, in terms of bargained-for exchange.*]
  A. Elements of Exchange—Performance and Promises
    1. Performances—[*Define performances that can be part of a bargained-for exchange, such as by identifying the kinds of things that amount to a performance, including acts and forbearances. You might also comment on the extent to which, if any, the performance must visit any detriment on the performing party, if you studied this.*]
      a. Acts—[*Identify common kinds of acts that can amount to a performance, or could be promised as a future performance.*]
        i. [*In one or more subsections at this level, provide examples of affirmative acts that are accepted as, or assumed to be, valid performances in cases you have studied.*]
      b. Forbearances—[*Identify examples of forbearances that can amount to a performance. Alternatively, if you studied a type of forbearance that was challenged in litigation, you can state a rule that helps to resolve when the forbearance amounts to a performance.*]
        i. [*In subsections at this level, illustrate your examples or your rule stated in subsection b immediately above, with the facts and results of cases that discuss whether a forbearance amounted to a performance and satisfied the consideration requirement.*]
    2. Promises—[*Define the commitment needed for a valid promise, as contrasted with an illusory promise.*]
      a. [*In subsections at this level, illustrate your rule about illusory promises with the critical facts and results of real or hypothetical cases.*]
  B. Bargained-for: Reciprocal Inducement—[*Define this requirement of bargained-for exchange.*]
    1. [*In subsections at this level or below, provide factually specific case illustrations of your definition of reciprocal inducement. If you studied problems related to reciprocal inducement—like conditional gratuitous promises, sham transactions, the problem of past performance for a subsequent*]

promise, or inducement as a test for "adequacy" of consideration—you might state a rule about one or more of those topics at this level, while illustrating them with cases one level down.]

C. Moral Obligation Theory—*[If you studied this, define the circumstances in which some courts will expand consideration beyond bargained-for exchange to enforce a promise given in recognition of the moral obligation arising out of a past performance. Use subsections below to illlustrate your rule with real or hypothetical cases.]*

VI. FLOWCHARTS AND OTHER GRAPHICS

In addition to outlining the course material, you might find that you can restate some of the rules in vivid and accessible fashion with a more graphic visual aid. Place no limits on your creativity. If you can think of a novel way to graphically illustrate a legal point, put it down on paper; you likely will remember the point precisely because you created an original graphic to illustrate it.

One popular example is a flowchart that uses a series of boxes and arrows to show how a multifaceted rule leads from one decision point to another, with forks leading to conclusions or more questions, depending on what answer is provided for a question stated in the previous box. The examples later in this chapter were produced with simple tools from Microsoft Word, showing that you need not earn a degree in graphic design to create boxes and insert arrows. Students with more computer savvy doubtlessly can produce outlines with more interesting graphics.

A. An Illustration from International Sales Law

As a simple example of creating illustrations, consider the text of two parallel provisions of the U.N. Convention on Contracts for the International Sale of Goods (CISG), articles 49 and 64:

CISG art. 49:
(1) The buyer may declare the contract avoided:
(a) if the failure by the seller to perform any of his obligations under the contract or this Convention amounts to a fundamental breach of contract; . . . .

CISG art. 64:
(1) The seller may declare the contract avoided:
(a) if the failure by the buyer to perform any of his obligations under the contract or this Convention amounts to a fundamental breach of contract; . . . .

You will learn from class discussion and other reading that "avoiding" a contract is a means of canceling the contract and one's own obligations under it. And as you can see from CISG articles 49 and 64, one ground for avoidance by either the buyer or the seller is a fundamental breach by the other party. Fundamental breach, in turn, is defined in article 25:

> **CISG art. 25:** A breach of contract committed by one of the parties is fundamental if it results in such detriment to the other party as substantially to deprive him of what he is entitled to expect under the contract, unless the party in breach did not foresee and a reasonable person of the same kind in the same circumstances would not have foreseen such a result.

The second clause in article 25, beginning with "unless," rather awkwardly states the foreseeability standard in negative terms. But you will learn in class that the phrasing of this second clause invites courts or arbitration tribunals to shift the burden of proof. If the buyer establishes a substantial deprivation of its expectations, the burden shifts to the seller to prove that it reasonably did not foresee this result.

CISG article 49 states other grounds for avoidance of a contract, but let's isolate the ground of fundamental breach to illustrate how that branch of avoidance could be represented in a simple flowchart.

This flowchart provides a good overview of the relationship between avoidance and fundamental breach, and it places the CISG article numbers in conspicuous places. On the other hand, if you take an upper level course that focuses on international sales law, you would encounter a great deal more detail on the topic of avoidance under CISG articles 49 and 64, more than would comfortably fit within a flow chart on a standard sheet of paper.

For example, excluded from the earlier quoted excerpts of CISG art. 49 and 64, and from the flowchart, are

- subsection (1)(b) of articles 49 and 64, which provides a second ground for avoidance, and
- subsection (2), which sets forth alternative prerequisites for avoidance relating to timing in various contexts.

Accordingly, the title of the flowchart above shows that the chart addresses only one ground for avoidance. To reveal all the grounds and requirements under articles 49 and 64, you could add two more branches to the top box in the flowchart, each of which would add several more boxes, and you might even succeed in fitting it all on one page.

If the flowchart becomes too cluttered when crammed into a single page, however, it may cease to provide an effective overview. You could address that challenge by creating three separate flowcharts, each on a separate page and each showing at a glance the elements of a ground for avoidance or the time limitations for declaring avoidance. And you might even consider placing the entire set of charts onto a single oversized sheet of paper or poster board.

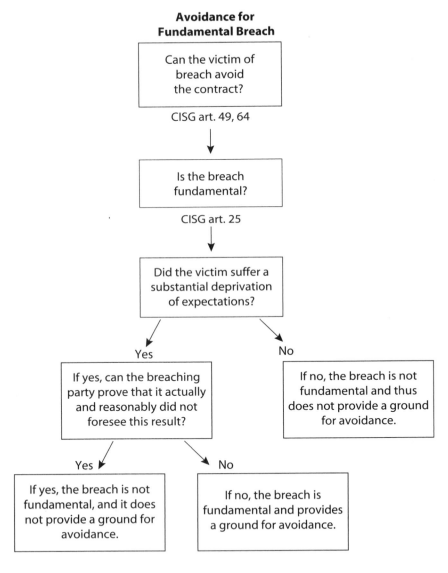

Still, if your studies include decisions from courts or arbitration tribunals interpreting these CISG articles, your flowchart would need to expand further if you hoped to illustrate the concepts with case summaries. Accordingly, if you find flowcharts to be useful, you probably should prepare them as a supplement to written outlines rather than as a replacement. Your outlines can address the law and illustrative cases fairly comprehensively, while your flowchart can serve as a visual overview of the basics, allowing you to see the "big picture" at a glance.

B. An Illustration from First-Year Contracts

This combined approach of outline supplemented by flowchart could work well with the complicated provisions of UCC § 2-207, a challenging topic of study in most first-year Contracts courses. This section of the Uniform Commercial Code overrules the common law mirror-image rule in sales of goods by recognizing contract formation in some circumstances even when the acceptance includes terms not found in the offer.

Initially, you will do well simply to understand the purpose of each of the three subsections of section 2-207. Read the provisions below, and try to determine the general issue addressed by each subsection numbered 1-3, and how those subsections relate to one another.

U.C.C. § 2-207. Additional Terms in Acceptance or Confirmation

(1) A definite and seasonable expression of acceptance or a written confirmation which is sent within a reasonable time operates as an acceptance even though it states terms additional to or different from those offered or agreed upon, unless acceptance is expressly made conditional on assent to the additional or different terms.

(2) The additional terms are to be construed as proposals for addition to the contract. Between merchants such terms become part of the contract unless:

    (a) the offer expressly limits acceptance to the terms of the offer;

    (b) they materially alter it; or

    (c) notification of objection to them has already been given or is given within a reasonable time after notice of them is received.

(3) Conduct by both parties which recognizes the existence of a contract is sufficient to establish a contract for sale although the writings of the parties do not otherwise establish a contract. In such case the terms of the particular contract consist of those terms on which the writings of the parties agree, together with any supplementary terms incorporated under any other provisions of this Act.

Did you figure out the purpose of each subsection? A flowchart at a high level of generality can show the basic relationship between these subsections without getting bogged down in the details of section 2-207:

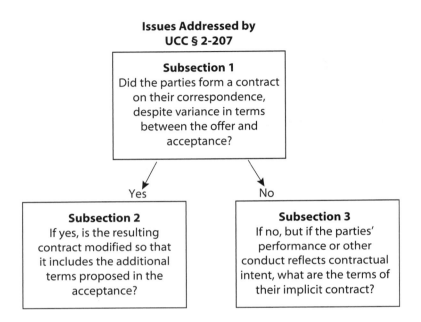

This basic structure of section 2-207, accessible from a glance at the flowchart above, is a valuable starting point for your study of this section. But, it is only a starting point, because each of these subsections presents a number of puzzles that, taken together, would fill a very complicated flowchart. Accordingly, you might be content to limit your flowchart to the basic information above and to address the details of section 2-207 in your outline.

Alternatively, you might supplement your outline and the overview flowchart above with a separate, more detailed flowchart for each of the three subsections. For example, you could devise a flowchart isolating the decision points in subsection 1.

Even this more focused flowchart omits a statutory reference to confirmations, which the statute should have addressed in a separate clause. The flowchart would require a separate set of branches to clearly convey confirmations. Better yet, you might address confirmations in a second, separate flowchart for subsection 1, to ensure that each flowchart remains uncluttered. Again, you might consider pasting all of your section 2-207 flowcharts on a sheet of posterboard, so that you can start with a broad overview, move to each successive flowchart that addresses the details of a subsection, and retain the ability to move your eyes from one subsection's flowchart to another.

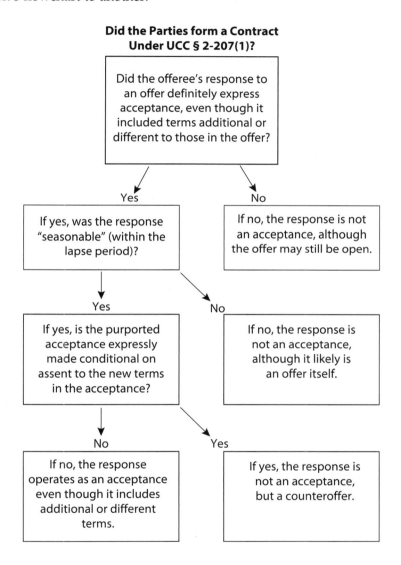

Did the Parties form a Contract Under UCC § 2-207(1)?

Did the offeree's response to an offer definitely express acceptance, even though it included terms additional or different to those in the offer?

Yes

If yes, was the response "seasonable" (within the lapse period)?

No

If no, the response is not an acceptance, although the offer may still be open.

Yes

If yes, is the purported acceptance expressly made conditional on assent to the new terms in the acceptance?

No

If no, the response is not an acceptance, although it likely is an offer itself.

No

If no, the response operates as an acceptance even though it includes additional or different terms.

Yes

If yes, the response is not an acceptance, but a counteroffer.

But remember, you don't need to fit all the details of a topic in your flowchart. You should limit your flowchart to critical decision points so that you can see the basics at a glance. Other details, such as how confirmations fit into section 2-207, are better left to your outline. And, of course, case law that interprets and applies section 2-207, or classroom hypotheticals that illustrate its application, are an important part of your outline and may not fit into your flowchart.

Note the much greater level of detail in the following outline, which can be supplemented with companion flowcharts:

I. The Battle of the Forms in Sales of Goods: UCC § 2-207—This section overrules the common law mirror-image rule for sales of goods, and it sets forth rules for determining the content of the contract.

A. Contract Formation on Correspondence with Varying Terms— Under subsection 1, a response to an offer "operates as an acceptance," even if it includes terms that are additional to or different from those in the offer, if the response definitely and seasonably expresses acceptance, and if it does not expressly make the acceptance conditional on assent to the new terms.

1. Definite Expression of Acceptance—The response must unequivocally express assent to the offer.

a. Example: In *Comco*, a response to an offer stating "we will give prompt attention to your order" did not definitely express acceptance because it was consistent with further consideration of the offer to determine whether to accept.

b. Caveat: Even if a response stated without equivocation "we accept," it is doubtful that it would operate as an acceptance under section 2-207(1) if it varied a term on which the parties had been specifically negotiating and had been unable to reach agreement, or if the response referred to a wildly different subject matter or quantity, such as definitely agreeing to sell an automobile when the offer offered to purchase 20 laptop computers.

2. Seasonable Expression of Acceptance—UCC § 1-204 defines "seasonably" as within the time agreed, or if no time is agreed, within a reasonable time, which is a traditional definition of the time before which an offer lapses.

3. Confirmations—Section 2-207(1) also refers to a "written confirmation which is sent within a reasonable time" as operating as an acceptance, but Official Comments 1 and 6 logically refer to confirmations as correspondence that confirm agreements already concluded, where acceptance has taken place. One reasonable interpretation: A confirmation that includes additional or different terms does not amount to a repudiation of the agreement previously formed, absent an express condition requiring assent to the new terms.

a. Example: In *Office Supply v. KCSB*, a seller's invoices "were effective to confirm the parties' agreement ... despite" an additional term.

b. Example: In *Step-Saver*, the court apparently treated the box top license within the delivered package to be a confirmation of an existing contract.

4. Acceptance Expressly Conditional—

. . .

B. Terms of an Agreement Recognized Under Subsection 1—Subsection 2 provides that additional terms in the acceptance or confirmation are proposals to modify the contract formed under subsection 1.

1. If at Least One Party is a Non-Merchant—Subsection 2 does not address the inclusion of additional terms when at least one party is not a merchant; presumably, normal principles of assent under section 2-204 and common law, requiring an affirmative manifestation of assent, would apply.

2. If both parties are merchants, then subsection 2 provides special rules that allow the additional terms in the acceptance to automatically be included in the contract, even without affirmative assent by the original offeror, subject to three exceptions: . . . .

. . .

C. If the parties' writings do not establish a contract, but their conduct "recognizes the existence of a contract," then they are contractually bound by "those terms on which the writings of the parties agree, together with" UCC default terms.

. . .

C. Don't Force a Flexible Analysis into a Mechanical Flowchart

Some legal issues lend themselves to flexible analysis based on factors that may appear in different combinations in different cases. For example, although the test for fundamental breach under the CISG contains two elements, defining decision points for the first flowchart in this chapter, the similar doctrine of material breach under the common law invites courts to apply a more flexible analysis. To determine whether a breach is material under the common law, courts weigh a number of factors relating to such things as the magnitude of the breach, the ability of the victim of breach to protect its interests by maintaining the contract and retaining a claim for damages, the possibility that the breaching party can cure the breach, and the likelihood that the breaching party will breach again. Not every one of these and other relevant factors will be in play in every case, so the balancing of factors can vary with each dispute. In one case, factors A and B might point moderately toward a minor breach but be outweighed by factors C, D, and E, which strongly point toward material breach. In another case, factor A might point toward material breach but be outweighed by factors C and D, which point toward minor breach, and with factors B and E contributing little or nothing to the analysis on the facts.

In an outline, you can describe such an analysis and list potentially relevant factors, and you can illustrate your description with factually rich examples from judicial decisions or classroom hypotheticals. However, a flexible weighing of factors does not lend itself to a traditional flowchart with decision points. Perhaps you can think of a way to graphically portray the flexible analysis, such as with factors spread through overlapping circles, themselves organized into a larger circular array, suggesting a sort of holistic analysis that responds to an issue identified in the center. Or, as a supplement to your outline, maybe you'll picture a balance scale with factors hovering above it in the center, ready to fall to one side or another of the balance. Feel free to be creative so that your graphic representation is meaningful and memorable to you.

Remember, however, that you will express your essay exam answer in prose, rather than graphics. Therefore, a flowchart or other graphic works best to help you visualize a legal analysis in its broad contours, and perhaps to puzzle through the elements of a legal test at the outset. After you create the graphic to help you fully comprehend a topic, express your understanding in writing, such as in outline form, which normally will allow you to work with the concepts in greater depth and detail.

VII. THE NEXT STEP

You will steadily acquire a working knowledge of the material in each of your courses throughout the semester, culminating in a course outline and related short outlines and checklists. You will then be ready to take the final steps in exam preparation: researching the kinds of exams that your professor tends to give and taking practice exams for that course. For more on those topics, proceed to the next chapter.

CHAPTER 7

Know Your Audience

In your Legal Writing course, you will learn to adapt the substance and style of your writing to meet the needs of your audience. What and how you write will differ depending on whether you are writing an office memorandum to educate a supervising attorney, an advice letter to a client untrained in the law, or a brief to advocate your client's position to a court.

Likewise, when preparing for exams, you should recognize that your professors will give different types of exams and will award points for different kinds of responses. This book introduces you to a variety of exam styles and identifies techniques that will help you do your best on any type of exam, assuming that you have diligently studied in the manner described in earlier chapters of this book. Nonetheless, you likely will derive additional advantages by educating yourself about the style and nature of the exams that each of your professors tends to give and about the kinds of responses that he or she most wants to see.

I. FIND AND STUDY PAST EXAMS

If your professor has previous final exams and model answers on file in the library or online, take the time to examine them carefully. After reviewing past exams, determine whether your professor tends to give essay questions, multiple-choice questions, or a combination of these or other types of questions. You might not have access to multiple-choice or other objective questions, because your professor might wish to reuse them; however, the exam instructions likely will describe all elements of the exam.

Additional inquiries focusing on essay questions might reveal valuable information:

- Do the essay questions each raise a single issue and call for a relatively short answer, or—as is traditional—do they set forth a lengthy fact pattern and call for full discussion of several issues?

- Do the questions ask you to argue both sides of each disputed issue, or (much less commonly) to advocate for one party only?
- Do the questions explicitly identify one or more issues for discussion, or (more typically) do they invite you in a more general fashion to "fully discuss the rights and liabilities of the parties," thus leaving it to you to identify issues for discussion?
- Is the exam a traditional "closed-book" exam, or do the instructions permit you to bring and consult your statutory supplement and, perhaps, other materials such as your notes and outlines?

You can gain further valuable information by studying the model answer to a past essay question and comparing it to your own answer:

- Does the model answer suggest that the professor typically has a single correct conclusion in mind so that your burden is to thoughtfully explain why and how the law applies to the facts to reach that result, or does it present reasonable arguments for both sides of a close question, leading to the selection of either of two reasonable conclusions?
- Does the model answer suggest that the professor expects you to cite— or even to explicitly analogize and distinguish—cases that you have studied in class and to quote relevant statutory text? Or does the model answer summarize the generally accepted majority rule, without citation to authority, before applying it to the facts; indeed, does the length of the question and the modest time allotted to it suggest that no greater detail in the statement of the legal rule would be feasible?

Once you have answered these questions, you can adapt your exam technique to conform to the characteristics of a good answer preferred by each of your professors. You might even want to secure this information early in the semester so that you can plan accordingly, adapting your study and review techniques to the requirements of each course's exam.

II. ASK YOUR PROFESSOR ABOUT THE EXAM

If your professor does not have prior exams and model answers on file, you should not feel shy about asking if he or she would be willing to spend a few minutes in class, or even an hour in a separate workshop, discussing the anticipated structure of his or her exam and the general kinds of answers that likely will earn a high score. If you are lucky, the professor might even consent to create and distribute a sample exam for the class.

Your professor likely will assume that all topics in the course are potential subjects of examination, so you normally will not advance your inquiry by asking questions about which topics will be covered on the exam. Asking about the general nature of the exam and the kind of answers that the professor seeks, however, should elicit a helpful response from most professors; after all, they should welcome the opportunity to increase the extent to which the exam answers will conform to their views of exam technique, so that they can base their grades on students' knowledge of the law and their display of analytic skills.

III. TAKE PRACTICE EXAMS AND ASSESS YOUR PERFORMANCE

A. Practice Makes Perfect

Imagine studying tennis with an expert instructor, and diligently practicing your serves and volleys over hours of drills, but never actually playing a full practice game with your instructor or a fellow student before entering your first competitive match. Even though you might have perfected the techniques of your serve, your forehand and backhand swings, and your movement on the court, you will not gain familiarity with the rules, tempo, strategy, and pressures of competition until you play practice games against a worthy opponent.

Similarly, no matter how diligently you study, outline, and review your course material during the regular semester, and no matter how well you comprehend the advice in the following chapters on exam techniques, you will not perfect your exam technique until you take practice exams. Only then can you identify deficits in your technique that need to be addressed.

For example, do you tend to rush through the fact statements, basing your analysis on a misunderstanding of the facts? Do you have an impulse to rush to a conclusion without fully discussing its legal and factual premises and arguing both sides? When confronted with two or more questions and a single allotment of time, are you prone to discussing the first question at excessive length, leaving no time to address the second question? You are not likely to have reliable answers to questions such as these unless you put yourself to the test.

Accordingly, you should squarely confront the law school examination process in a practice setting, early enough in the semester so that you still have time to improve your technique and adjust your study habits before the final exam. Every hour of practice will help expose your weaknesses, provide you with opportunities to improve, and increase the level of experience, confidence, and expertise that you bring to your first midterm or final exam. It is much less likely that you will be hampered by an intense fear of the unknown if your first law school exam is a familiar experience. Accordingly, do not delay in completing your study of exams in this book, outlining a completed unit in one of your courses, and taking a practice or past exam that addresses material in that unit.

To make your first law school exam a familiar experience, you should take practice exams under realistic conditions. If your professor offers a practice exam in a formal exam setting, take full advantage of this opportunity, studying for it in the same way you would a final exam, and focusing your intellectual energies during the exam as though your entire grade depended on the outcome. If no practice exam is offered, find a past exam from that course on file in the library or online, and mimic the official exam procedures as much as possible when you take the exam. If you take the practice exam at home, eliminate all distractions and adhere strictly to the time limits. If you take it with a study group, try to reserve a classroom or other examination room at your school, and take the exam together, perhaps with a fellow student calling out the start time, the five-minute mark before the end of the exam, the one-minute mark, and the end.

B. Solicit Feedback on Your Performance

You must hold yourself to high standards on practice exams, because your professor will certainly hold you to high standards on the final exam. If you have a model answer, compare your answer to it with a critical eye, and discuss the question and model answer with members of your study group who took the exam with you. Try to overcome any subconscious inclination to minimize the extent to which your answer falls short of the model answer; you will want to aggressively identify any deficits in your performance so that you can address them.

Indeed, to test your judgment whether differences between your answer and the model answer are significant, ask your professor if he or she would be willing to quickly read through your answer and provide a critique. To maximize the chances that your professor will take the time to do this, be prepared. Explain that you have carefully reviewed the model answer and have concluded that your answer could be improved in certain ways, and ask your professor if he or she can confirm the validity of your critique or add any other insights. At worst, your professor might respond that the model answer is the best guide and that providing you with a private critique would entitle all other students to the same service, at an excessive expenditure of the professor's time. At best, however, the professor will be delighted with your diligence and will take the time to provide you with invaluable insights about how he or she would have graded your answer and about the kinds of improvements that would maximize your score.

Of course, you are not ready early in the semester to respond to all of the questions on a past final exam, because you will not have completed your study of most of the issues raised by them. To get started, therefore, you might need to respond to a fact-based problem posed in your casebook or in class, relating to a topic that you have covered in class and reviewed.

Such a problem might be much easier than a typical final exam question, because it likely will be shorter and will address a single issue that is identified for you. A simple question, though, is a good starting place early in the semester; you will have time to tackle more challenging practice exams later in the semester, allowing you to apply lessons learned from earlier experiences.

C. Pose Your Own Exam Questions

If you have some extra time during the semester, use your familiarity with your course and with your professor's style of essay questions to create your own exam questions. Ask yourself, "If I were Professor X, what kind of question would I write to test students on these two topics, which were emphasized in class?" Then, try your hand at drafting such a question and answering it.

I am not suggesting that you will get very lucky and will guess the content of a question that appears on the exam; as discussed in the next section, attempted predictions of this sort might lead you to answer the question you hoped to find rather than the one that actually appears on the exam. I am suggesting only that this is a good study technique, for the following reason: Just as you must learn a subject very well before you can teach it, you can be certain that you know a topic of the law well, and that you have developed good analytic skills, if you can understand how your original fact pattern raises issues and would support arguments for either side under applicable law.

IV. TAKE THE EXAM AS WRITTEN (NOT AS YOU WISH IT WERE WRITTEN)

It is a fairly open "secret" in a very few courses that the professor does not like to create new essay questions each year, and that he or she annually repeats essentially the same question on a topic, perhaps with a few changes in names of characters or of other relatively insignificant events. When this is the case, studying and taking past exams can be very helpful indeed. You should recognize, however, that the professor almost certainly will cover his or her tracks by making some changes in the facts, even if the general structure of the question and the issues raised are very similar to those of a past exam on file. Thus, even in such a course, your answer will never be precisely the same as the best or model answer from a previous exam.

Much more commonly, the content of an examination will be very difficult to predict. Your professors are primarily interested in assessing your creative analytic skills rather than your ability to memorize someone else's analysis; consequently, most professors will try very hard to create new essay questions that raise different issues from those raised in recent exams; at the least, they will try to raise the issues in very different combinations or factual contexts. True, you can reasonably surmise that the professor will more likely draft a question around a topic that you studied in great detail over the course of several class hours than around some minor matter that occupied only a few minutes of class discussion. However, even that is only a probability rather than a certainty, only a basis for allocating study time and not for interpreting an exam question.

At most, after reviewing past exams from a period of three to five years, you might hope to identify the range of issues that the professor believes are suitable for testing with essay questions. For example, you might identify 30 issues that have appeared in essay exams over such a period, most of them appearing in one form or another on more than one exam, but no more than 15 of them appearing in any one exam. Perhaps such research will help provide you with a checklist of issues that you should study with special diligence; however, it would not allow you to predict which 12 or 15 will appear on the next exam, nor will it exclude the possibility of the professor writing a major question that focuses on an issue that never before appeared on an exam.

Thus, even though taking past or practice exams will greatly improve your ability to perform well on the final exam, you must not assume that your familiarity with past or practice exams will allow you to predict the issues that will be raised on the final exam. Beware of any tendency to address a topic on the exam simply because you have studied that topic thoroughly, have encountered it on past exams, and have generated a fervent hope that it will appear on the final exam. Most professors will give you no credit for even a terrific discussion of an issue that is not raised by the facts of the exam question.

In sum, past and practice exams will expose gaps in your knowledge of the law, help you identify deficits in your fact analysis and your exam technique, and thus help you address those gaps and deficits before the final exam. They are not, however, a reliable basis for predicting precisely which issues will be tested or what facts will be employed to raise the issues.

V. THE NEXT STEP

On the eve of your first exam, you probably will feel that you had too little time to prepare as thoroughly as you would have liked. If you are following the advice in this book, however, you will be as well prepared for exams as anyone could reasonably expect in light of time constraints. It is now time to take a deep breath, turn the page, and immerse yourself in the techniques of taking the exams.

PART FOUR

TAKING LAW SCHOOL EXAMS

At last, you have completed your preparation, and you are ready to take your exams. The following chapters provide invaluable advice on applying your newly acquired knowledge and skills to exam questions. Although this advice should be generally applicable to nearly all exams, remember that professors have substantial academic freedom to create their exams and grade them in whatever manner they see fit, underscoring the importance of the admonition in Chapter 7 to "know your audience" when you compose your answers. Accordingly, you can take the advice in the following chapters as a good starting point, but you should adapt this advice to suit the specific preferences of each of your professors, as revealed by past exams and model answers or by your professors' statements about the upcoming exam.

CHAPTER 8

Getting Primed for the Task

Chapters 9 through 12 address exam technique in great detail. First, however, you should reflect on the importance of mental attitude and physical health to your exam performance.

I. ADOPT A WINNING ATTITUDE

You have worked hard all semester. True, your confidence has been shaken once or twice, and you keep measuring yourself against that talkative student across the room who seems to know everything. However, if you have been listening carefully all semester and have developed critical analytic skills, you might be better prepared than that talkative student to do well on the final exams. Why not adopt a winning attitude and set high goals for yourself?

At the very least, a winning attitude means avoiding the self-defeating, defensive posture of creating excuses for failure. If you doubt your ability to do well on exams, you might fear that you will earn poor grades even after studying to the maximum degree possible, risking a blow to your ego. As a defensive measure, you might subconsciously allow yourself to be distracted from studying during the exam period, or even earlier in the semester, so that you can blame low grades on disruption of your study schedule rather than on a limited aptitude for the study of law.

Ironically, you can help avoid this trap partly by remembering that your value as a human being is not measured by your performance on law school exams. The exams are necessarily arbitrary to a certain degree, and they cannot measure the full range of skills and traits that translate into success in the practice of law. Beyond that, they obviously do not measure your qualities as a friend, parent, colleague, or citizen; moreover, a lack of aptitude for excelling in the study of law does not preclude success in other fields of study and practice.

By placing your study of law in proper perspective, you can moderate the pressure, freeing yourself to perform your best. No one will fault you if you spare no effort to do your best, even if the results fall short of your hopes and expectations. On the other hand, what a shame it will be if you squeak by after defensively limiting your opportunities to do well, and then spend your time wondering how much better you could have done had you pulled out all the stops.

Accordingly, you should vow to do your very best and to honor whatever result that effort produces. Because you cannot know before the exams are graded what your best efforts will produce, prepare for exams with the goal of clearly passing all your courses and even scoring near the top of the class. Although a top score might seem unlikely in light of the impressive credentials of your fellow students and the realities of the grading curve, you are more likely to rise to the top if you reach for the stars than if you stare at the ground in anticipation of defeat.

In fact, even if a winning attitude does not come easily to you, I recommend that you consciously convince yourself to adopt such an attitude. Approach your exam preparation with all the dedication and enthusiasm you can muster, and try to visualize successful completion of your outlines and success on the exams.

II. MAINTAIN YOUR MACHINE

Doing your best, however, does not mean adopting such a single-minded work ethic that you burn out emotionally and physically just before exams. A tired mind and body will not respond well to the rigors of a demanding three-hour exam.

Accordingly, your busy weekly schedule throughout the semester should include adequate time for sleep, exercise, a healthy diet, visits to the medical clinic, and contact with or phone calls to loved ones, whose support could be important to your emotional health during exams. You undoubtedly will need to sacrifice some favorite activities to make room for the immensely time-consuming endeavor of studying the law, but some basic needs must be met to ensure that you do not run out of gas a few dozen yards before the finish line.

In particular, you should avoid the exam-review technique favored by procrastinating college students: cramming all night before the exam, hoping to learn and retain critical information long enough to answer questions on the exam through sleepy eyes. The reading comprehension and analytic skills required for law school exams will not come easily to a student who has attempted to use an "all-nighter" to compensate for an earlier failure to study. Plan ahead, pace yourself, and come to the exam alert and well rested. In the best of situations, you can use the eve of the exam to review your outline and checklist of issues, rest your eyes and mind—maybe by listening to music, taking a walk, stretching, or meditating—and then get a good night's sleep.

Finally, take prudent measures to avoid getting sick during the exam period. Although most schools will allow you to reschedule exams if a major illness intervenes, a minor illness will simply rob you of energy. If you must take an exam with a minor cold or other routine ailment, do not assume that your grade will inevitably suffer and then use that as an excuse to perform half-heartedly; you often can summon the strength and determination to overcome minor discomfort in the exam room. Nonetheless, you can maximize your chances of being at the top of your game by taking precautions against catching a cold or flu at the end of the semester.

III. FACING EXAM DAY

Because so much seems to be riding on the outcome of your law school exams, you likely will feel intense pressure on exam day. A little nervousness is a good thing: It will help you to focus your attention and to read, analyze, and write more quickly and efficiently than in most other circumstances. Excessive nervousness, however, can hamper your ability to concentrate, and it might even cause you to panic and begin writing before you have properly analyzed a question. Accordingly, it pays to adopt measures that will help you enter the exam in a controlled, productive frame of mind.

This might sound corny, but the morning of an exam is a good time for some motivational music or mind-focusing meditation. Many years ago, before leaving my apartment to take law school exams, I customarily turned up the volume on my stereo system and played songs that tended to fill me with a sense of idealism and accomplishment. Yes, one could probably stage a humorous parody of this ritual, but it worked. It helped me build confidence, set lofty goals, and resolve to do everything possible to reach those goals.

Others might prefer exercise, meditation, prayer, inspirational poetry, or a pep talk with a supportive family member. Whatever method works for you, take some time to clear your mind of doubts, so that you walk into the exam room not with a sense of impending doom, but with confidence in your abilities.

Indeed, even if a high level of confidence is not entirely warranted by your experiences during the semester, generate an air of confidence from whatever level of preparation was feasible for you. Convince yourself to view the exams as welcome opportunities to show what you know, to match wits with your professor, to unravel the mysteries of their exam questions, and to beat them at their own game.

IV. THE NEXT STEP

It is now time to explore general techniques common to all exam questions.

CHAPTER 9

Techniques Common to All Essay Questions

Chapters 10 and 11 present detailed discussions of the substantive components of your answers to different kinds of essay questions. We begin in this chapter, however, with a few tips about techniques that are applicable to any form of essay question.

I. EFFECTIVE USE OF TIME

A. Expect Time Pressure

Managing your time during a law school exam is a surprisingly important component of good exam technique. As you will learn by taking practice exams during the semester, most in-class law school exams allow you substantially less time than would ordinarily be required to provide the best and most complete answer possible.

Some professors impose this time pressure to reward students who successfully identify and discuss only relevant matters, those raised by the law and by the facts of the problem. Although they do not deduct points for irrelevant discussion, every minute that a student spends discussing some matter not raised by the facts and law means less time for scoring points on relevant matters.

Time pressure on an exam also helps the professor measure skills of quick thinking and efficient writing, which some professors believe are important to the practice of law. Finally, many professors simply underestimate the time required for students to analyze the exam questions and write an excellent answer to each. For all these reasons, and probably others as well, you need to adopt a disciplined approach to allocating your time during a typical in-class exam.

B. Logical Allocation, Not Gambling

First, let's address some complications that might arise in allocating time between essay questions in one part of an exam and objective questions, such as multiple-choice questions, in another part. If both parts are given as a single exam, with a single allotment of time, you might be tempted to spend nearly all your time writing as much as possible on the essay portion, and then guessing on all the objective questions, marking your computer score sheet in the final few minutes of the exam.

I cannot imagine that such a strategy would maximize a student's scores except under very unusual circumstances, but you should not even to be tempted to adopt such an approach, and your grades should not depend on whether you adopted a winning strategy regarding the optimal allocation of time between the essay and objective questions. When I administer exams that include both essay questions and multiple-choice questions, I customarily break up the exam into two separate parts, with a specified time allotted for the essay questions, which are collected before the objective question sheets are distributed under a separate time allotment.

If your professor, however, imposes a single allotment of time for both essay and objective questions, I recommend that you follow the exam's suggested time allocation between those parts of the exam, or—if the exam does not provide a time recommendation—that you allocate your time in a manner that is consistent with actually analyzing the objective questions rather than guessing the answers in the last few minutes. The factors associated with adopting some other kind of "gaming" strategy are too variable to provide a basis for further guidance on such a risky approach. Let's therefore assume that you are allocating time between essay questions under a single time allotment for all the essays, or between objective questions under a separate time allotment.

C. Objective Questions

Your strategy is simple for an exam or exam part that consists entirely of objective questions of the same nature, such as all multiple-choice questions or all true–false questions. Start with an equal allotment of time for each question by dividing the number of questions into the total time allowed. Thus, if you have 90 minutes to complete 30 multiple-choice questions, you should allow yourself an average of three minutes for each.

I refer to an average time per question because the questions might vary considerably in length and difficulty. Thus, your ability to answer one question in half the allotted time per question will leave you extra time for a difficult question that incorporates a long fact pattern. If you check the time after every five or ten questions on such an exam, and confirm that you are proceeding at the average rate, then you will know that you are on track. If you are well ahead of that pace, you might want to consider whether you are rushing your reading and analysis of each question and should take more time to answer with care. Conversely, if you are lagging behind the required pace, you should recognize that you likely will be leaving the final few questions to guesswork unless you can proceed at a faster rate.

D. Essay Questions

At the beginning of any essay portion of an examination, you should determine how much time you will allocate to each question and then adhere to that schedule. Adequate discussion of all the questions in an examination generally will score more points than unusually thorough discussions of only some of the questions at the cost of inadequate treatment of others. The same holds true for treatment of issues within a question: Adequate discussion of all the major issues will generally score more points than an unusually thorough discussion of only half the issues raised by a question.

1. An Illustration in a Nonlegal Setting

By way of illustration, imagine that a friend has three tables and twelve chairs for an outdoor dinner party and has asked you to set them up for twelve hosts and guests, who will be sitting down for a dinner that must be served in 30 minutes. Allotting ten minutes for each table, you might have time to set up each table, slide the tables into reasonably logical positions on the patio, place four chairs at each table (the maximum number that can fit comfortably), throw a tablecloth on each table, and—racing in the final minutes—just manage to place a plate, napkin, and set of silverware on the table in front of each chair, with the knife, fork, and spoon all set on top of the napkin. A few moments later, all the guests could take their places at the tables, eager to eat, and ready to provide you with their drink orders.

Alternatively, you could spend 30 minutes setting up a single table to perfection, positioning the table at the precise center of the patio, and covering it with a carefully selected tablecloth, the corners of which you could clip together to hold it tight to the table in case the breeze picks up. Although the folding chairs appear to be clean, you might take the time to wipe four chairs with a dustcloth before positioning them along the sides of the table. In front of each chair, you could place a table setting, with a fork on the left of the plate, a knife and spoon on the right, and an extra spoon at the top of the plate for dessert or coffee. After finding four cloth napkins that match the tablecloth, you might fold each napkin into an interesting shape that allows it to stand out in the center of each plate. You could also place a water glass, white wine glass, and red wine glass at each place setting, to accommodate various beverages that might be served. Finally, if you find a suitable vase, you could fill it with water and gather some cheery flowers from the garden. You could then place the vase on the table and arrange the flowers just as the first four guests arrive at the patio to take their seats at the table. They would be delighted with your handiwork. Of course, eight other hungry guests would approach the patio with puzzled looks on their faces.

The single table setting described in the second scenario might be optimal for all three tables if you had the time to set up all three in that manner. Indeed, even if you realized that your host had provided you with insufficient time to set up all three in that fashion, you might still be tempted to set a single table in that grand fashion, just to display your capabilities.

Obviously, however, the host of the party would much prefer that you set up all three tables in some reasonable manner, so that all twelve guests can be comfortably accommodated as the dinner is being served. The benefits of momentarily delighting four guests would be outweighed by the inconvenience suffered by the remaining guests, by the delay in serving food that is starting to grow cold, and by the discomfort felt even by the four seated guests, who now realize that other guests had no place to sit and that the first table would need to be moved from the center of the patio to make room for the other two.

You might have felt frustrated by your lack of opportunity to set all three tables in optimum fashion; however, your friend provided you with sufficient time for the basics and no more, and your objective should be to meet your friend's expectations and desires. After all, adequate seating for all the guests can launch a successful dinner party, even if they are eating off of paper plates.

2. Application to the Legal Setting

Similarly, if you are writing a brief to an appellate court, arguing for reversal of the judgment in the trial court, you ordinarily will represent your client best by adequately presenting all of the two, three, or four solid arguments for reversal that you have developed from your research and analysis. If you exhaust the page limit of the brief by presenting only one of those arguments in great detail, you will waive the other arguments, and you likely will present the single argument at greater length than is necessary to get your point across to the court. Because you cannot predict which of these arguments will most appeal to the judges on the appellate court, you will be gambling that the single argument you present is the one most likely to win a reversal. To be sure, you will not want to waste the court's time, or the space within your page limitation, with numerous additional arguments that are weak or of questionable relevance;

however, an adequate presentation of the central arguments will place those grounds for reversal squarely before the court and will set the stage for oral argument.

Most essay exams will be graded in a manner that is consistent with these illustrations. If a professor intends to raise three major issues in an exam question, he or she likely will provide you with a generous amount of credit for spotting an issue, summarizing the basic contours of the applicable rules, and displaying at least a brief analysis of the facts, all in a reasonably well-organized manner. If you develop your answer to an issue in greater detail, you might earn a higher score on that single issue, but likely at a diminishing rate.

So, for example, let's assume that you are answering a question for which a total of 60 minutes is allotted, and you have spent 15 minutes reading and analyzing the question, identifying three issues to discuss, and briefly outlining your discussion of those three issues on scratch paper. For the remaining 45 minutes, you will write out your analysis of the issues in a logically organized fashion. If the three issues are roughly equal in difficulty, the professor presumably would expect you to spend about 15 minutes writing on each issue. Let's also assume that your professor will award you raw points for relevant statements and arguments in your exam answer, and has allocated approximately 15 points for each of the three issues in this first question.

In these circumstances, you likely would earn most or all of the 15 points allocated to the first issue by setting forth as complete an analysis of that issue as the professor might expect would be feasible in 15 minutes. If you went beyond that, however, and expended an additional ten minutes discussing this first issue in greater detail, you likely would not continue earning points at an average rate of one per minute, because your professor's grading plan might contemplate giving a designated maximum number of points for a particular issue, perhaps 15 to 20. Thus, additional points beyond a certain range might be more difficult to earn.

So, if you spent an extra ten minutes—a total of 25 minutes—striving for the perfect answer to the first issue, you might manage to coax an additional four points from the professor by making relevant supplementary observations or arguments, for a total of 19 points. If you then spent all 20 minutes of your remaining time discussing just the second issue, you might earn an additional 16 points, for a grand total of 35 raw points. By not even addressing the third issue, however, you would have robbed yourself of the opportunity to earn points for the "low-hanging fruit" of that issue: the basic legal standards and obvious factual arguments that you could have presented without hesitation or head-scratching. Had you allocated your 45-minute writing time evenly among the three issues, you would have been in good position to earn close to 45 total raw points.

I must concede that this example is simplified for purposes of illustration. Not all professors use an objective point system as they grade, and some of them might actually provide you with a single-issue question and sufficient time to write an answer that is the equivalent of the grand table setting. Other professors might be more generous than I have suggested in their scoring of an answer that does a terrific job of analyzing one or two issues, even though it leaves at least one issue unaddressed or inadequately addressed.

Still, as a general matter, my point is valid: You usually will score most highly by addressing all significant issues raised by an exam question, even if time pressure requires you to present your answer to each issue in a somewhat abbreviated fashion. For the same reasons, you are likely to score more points if you present an adequate treatment of all questions in an exam than if you answer one question in great detail but leave one or more questions unanswered. You should be guided by this generalization unless your research of past exams or your discussions with your professor reveal that he or she cares more about your ability to analyze at least one issue in great depth than about your ability to identify and adequately discuss all significant issues.

3. Allocating Your Time Among Essay Questions

Under this generalization, you should be prepared to wrap up your discussion on an essay question, or an issue within an essay question, and proceed to the next one, even if you are bursting with additional things to say. Allocating your time in this manner might require some discipline, but you must accept the fact that your professor often will not provide you with sufficient time to do all that might otherwise be possible. If necessary, you can spend 30 seconds sketching your remaining thoughts on an issue, in outline form in your exam answer sheet, before proceeding to the next issue or question.

To allocate your time effectively, first note the time the exam commences and the total time allotted for the essay exam or for the essay part of the exam if that is being administered separately. Calculate and write down the ending time for the whole exam or the part that is being administered, and then quickly look through the essay questions to arrive at a reasonable time allotment for answering each question. If the exam itself recommends a certain allocation of time among essay questions, that provides an easy and relatively reliable guide to follow, because it likely corresponds to the grading weights that the professor will apply to the questions. (But quickly add up the separate recommended times to ensure that their sum is equal to the total exam time. Professors have been known to make silly addition mistakes, which are best cleared up with the exam administrator as soon as possible.) If the exam does not include a recommended time allocation, devise your own allocation—and try to stick to it—based on your quick assessment of the length and difficulty of each essay question. Then, as you later analyze each question, make sure that you at least make a mental note of the time that you believe should be allocated to each issue raised by the question.

So, for example, you might first write in your notes, as the administrator's instructions are ending, that a three-hour examination is getting underway at 8:45 a.m. and thus will end at 11:45 a.m. When you are given the signal to begin the exam, you might then quickly discover that the exam presents two essay questions that are moderate in length, followed by two substantially longer ones. Because the questions do not come with suggested time allocations, you make a rough determination that you should spend about 30 minutes each on the two shorter questions, and one hour each on the two long questions. You thus mark the approximate times for completion of each question: 9:15 A.M., 9:45 A.M., 10:45 A.M., and 11:45 A.M. Similarly, once you read the first question and determine that it raises two substantial issues, you might decide to spend about six minutes carefully reading and analyzing the question, and then 12 minutes writing your analysis of each issue.

Your self-imposed time limits, of course, are imprecise markers based on a glance at the whole exam and then on your first reading of each question; you can adjust them a bit as you go. Nonetheless, the initial time limits should serve to remind you along the way that you need to move to the next issue or the next question before you get bogged down. To return to the example of the dinner party, you generally will be better off setting three tables in a reasonable manner than using all your time to set one table in spectacular fashion, leaving most of the dinner guests without a place to sit.

E. Never Give Up

If you find yourself confused by a question, stick to your time limits, but do not give up trying to unravel the problem. If you find yourself stalled on a question despite being well prepared for the exam, do not panic: It is highly likely that other students are stalled as well. Do not give in to anger, frustration, resentment, or self-pity. Just keep thinking, perhaps from different angles, while breaking the problem into manageable pieces, and give it your best shot within the time limits. You might surprise yourself and experience an intellectual breakthrough in the final few minutes, allowing you to distinguish yourself with at least a skeletal analysis.

II. READING AND ANALYZING ESSAY QUESTIONS

Although law school examinations require quick thinking, uninterrupted concentration, and rapid writing, you should not begin writing your answers prematurely. As already recommended, for example, you should spend a few moments allocating your time between questions before you even begin the exam in earnest. Beyond that, you are more likely to write well-organized and analytically sound responses—without substantial corrections and other wasted effort—if you devote up to a quarter of the time allotted for each question to understanding the facts and planning your answer. Occasionally, a professor might give a question that requires an unusual amount of reading and thinking but not a commensurately exceptional amount of writing, in which case you might benefit by spending up to a third or even half of the allotted time on these prewriting tasks.

A. Mastering the Question

1. A Plan of Action

Through taking past and practice exams, you might develop an approach to reading essay questions that suits your personal style. The following approach works for me and likely is a good starting place for you as well.

Read the exam question once at a moderately quick pace to get a very general picture of the events described, to classify the general nature of the probable claims and defenses, and to discover the particular direction or question posed by the professor, the "call of the question," which usually appears at the end of the problem. This "quick read" will help you narrow the topics of the question to certain categories, enabling you to more effectively explore the facts in detail in a second reading of the question.

If the essay question extends for more than a page or so, you might want to start by skipping ahead to the end of the question to look for the call of the question, even before proceeding with your initial quick read-through. The specific directions there might provide you with an orientation that will increase the efficiency of your initial, quick read.

Either way, once you have completed your quick read and have a general picture of the nature of the question, you should then read the problem at least once again, this time at a much more deliberate pace. Your objective now is to spot specific issues and to make marks or margin notes that highlight important facts that will be relevant to the discussion of the issues.

Take great care to avoid missing or misreading one or more facts. Even a student with an exceptional knowledge of the law can lose an armful of points by applying that impressive knowledge to the wrong facts. Although you are working under considerable time pressure, you will only lose further ground by paying inadequate attention to the facts.

2. An Illustration

Let's walk through the plan of action with the following sample essay question:

> Kelly is an anesthesiologist who is employed and paid a salary by Samaritan, a private hospital. When Rose's orthopedic surgeon scheduled Rose for

surgery at Samaritan to correct a bone deformity in Rose's foot, Samaritan assigned Kelly to administer general anesthesia. Kelly informed Rose of the advantages and risks associated with the three most appropriate general anesthetics. On the basis of relative costs, Rose rejected the safest but most expensive anesthetic, forane, in favor of a generally safe and more widely used anesthetic, ethane.

Although Samaritan protocols require anesthesiologists to administer general anesthesia only when assisted by qualified medical personnel, prior to the surgery Kelly administered the general anesthesia to Rose without assistance, before the surgical team had arrived and while the circulating nurse was occupied with another patient. While administering general anesthesia, Kelly concentrated intensely on gauges on the equipment that measured Rose's intake of the anesthetic. Kelly did not maintain visual contact with Rose or with equipment monitoring Rose's vital signs; as a consequence, Kelly failed to terminate the intake of the anesthetic until ten seconds after the first visible signs of an adverse reaction. Sophisticated medical tests later showed that Rose suffered from a rare and previously undiagnosed disorder of the nervous system that produced a severe reaction to the anesthetic, causing her heart to stop. Although Rose was ultimately resuscitated, she suffered permanent brain damage because of an interruption of flow of oxygen to the brain during the heart stoppage.

Fully discuss all issues arising out of a claim that Samaritan is liable to Rose in tort. Do not discuss remedies.

You undoubtedly have noticed that this essay question is largely a collection of facts with a general direction to discuss the issues. If you had studied tort law, you would be familiar with the legal basis for tort liability and would recognize ways in which the facts would raise debatable questions about whether the various elements of a legal basis for liability are satisfied. If you were armed with that knowledge, you could discern from a quick reading of the facts that the question deals generally with possible negligence in the form of medical malpractice, rather than some other basis for tort liability that you had studied, such as fraud, trespass, or intentional infliction of emotional distress. So, with even a quick glance at the facts, you have narrowed the focus of your inquiry and analysis.

The call of the question in the final paragraph both broadens and narrows the scope of your answer. It specifically instructs you to exclude remedies from your analysis, so you will not need to spend time writing about the kinds of damages that Rose might recover for her injuries. It also asks you to assume that Rose will make any claim against Samaritan, not Kelly. Otherwise, however, the question simply asks you to "fully discuss all issues," a direction that delegates to you the task of identifying issues, and that invites you to discuss both sides of the dispute, rather than advocate for one party only.

So far, you have assimilated this very general information after a quick glance at the question and have focused attention on the call of the question, taking less than a minute of your precious time. At this point, you should go back and read the question carefully, looking for issues (legal and factual matters that could be reasonably disputed) and making marks or margin notes next to facts that raise the issues and that can be used to argue for one side or another.

For example, you see that the question contains numerous facts regarding Kelly's actions in administering the anesthetic, some suggesting due care on her part and some suggesting carelessness. If you had studied torts, you would know that these facts raise a question about whether Kelly acted negligently, a basis for tort liability. Or, more to the point, these facts tip you off that your professor is trying hard to raise that issue and has given you facts to work with in arguing both sides of the issue. You also see facts that raise interesting questions about whether the injury was really caused by Kelly's actions or stems more from Rose's rare condition or her selection of the anesthetic. If you had studied torts, you might thus identify issues regarding the legal doctrine of causation and the defense of assumption of the risk. As you make these observations, you are identifying issues for discussion and are noting which facts will be relevant to your analysis of each issue.

In contrast, because the facts state that Samaritan employs Kelly on salary and assigned her to Rose's surgery, and that Kelly acted in the normal course of her employment at Samaritan, you decide that the issue of Samaritan's "vicarious" liability for Kelly's actions is not really debatable and will follow automatically from any tort claim that could be proved against Kelly. You thus have determined to address the matter of vicarious liability in no more than two sentences, leaving the bulk of your time to more fully discuss matters that are subject to greater debate. For example, you might use one sentence to state the rule for an employer's vicarious liability, otherwise known as *respondeat superior*, and another sentence stating your conclusion that Samaritan would be liable for Kelly's negligence, if any, and supporting that conclusion with a concise reference to the employment relationship.

B. Plan Your Answer

If you are really pressed for time, and especially if you are not a fast writer or typist, you might be tempted to begin writing your answer as soon as you have analyzed the question in the manner just described. You likely will write a better answer, however, and you might even save time during the writing process, if you take just a minute before you begin writing to jot down on scratch paper a brief outline of your answer.

The outline on scratch paper should be nothing more than a skeletal construction of the issues that you intend to address and the significant facts relating to each of those issues. The outline becomes your primary vehicle for analysis and organization, something to which you can return in the midst of writing out your answer, especially when you have completed discussion of a subissue and need a quick reminder of the big picture and the next logical link in the chain of analysis. More importantly, the outline forces you to think deeply about the analysis that was taking shape as you were reading the question the second time through. If something about your analysis or planned order of presentation does not make sense, you can more easily address the confusion at this preliminary outlining than at a later stage when you have written for 15 minutes and only then discover that you are headed toward a dead end.

To ensure that your outline provides the intended benefits but does not consume an inordinate amount of precious exam time, you should include just enough detail to help you think through the question and to provide yourself with a guide when you are writing your answer. Do not waste time by constructing an outline that is nearly as detailed as your fully written answer.

For example, the analysis of the sample examination question given earlier might result in the following informal outline of law and factual arguments, appearing only on your scratch paper:

> *Sam. —Negligence*
> *K is EE; vicarious liability*
> *Issue: Neg. act—*
> *Rule: med. standard of care*
>   *Facts for K/S: explained risks; monitored intake carefully*
>   *Facts for R: adm. alone (violating hosp. rules); did not monitor R or vital signs*
> *Issue: Prox. Cause—*
> *Rule: Supervening cause rule, but thin-skulled plaintiff rule*
>   *Facts for K/S: injury prim. caused by Rose's disorder, maybe injury occur even if K had monitored & stopped sooner*
> *Arg. for R: but negl. party should take victim as she finds her*
> *Defense—Assumption of risk—voluntary and knowing*
>   *Facts for K/S: R chose less safe ane. to save $*
>   *Facts for R: but did not assume risk of unsafe solo admin.*

Finally, after completing your outline, you should quickly read the problem one more time before beginning to write. After you have fully analyzed the problem in the outline, you can more effectively recognize the legal significance of facts in the problem. Sometimes, facts that appeared to be insignificant in earlier readings might now jump out at you as suitable support for a legally relevant argument.

C. Reacting to Apparent Mistakes in an Exam Question

Good essay questions are difficult to write, and your professor might change parts of them through successive drafts. With some regularity, an obvious typo or other error remains in the final draft. It might be a date that makes no sense, or the transposition of the names of two characters in one passage of a story, or your professor's changing a name throughout most of the exam question on second draft but neglecting to change it in one spot. Sometimes the difficulty is the simple omission of a fact that you need for an essential element of your analysis.

1. State Your Assumption About an Error or Omission

If you detect an obvious mistake in an exam, you should notify the exam administrator immediately if your school's procedures permit you to do so. The administrator might convey instructions to you about how to react, or might solicit a correction from the authoring professor.

If no guidance is available from the professor or an exam administrator, you should state your assumption about the correct fact and then analyze the problem accordingly. For example, you might state: "The call of the question asks for a discussion of Brown's potential liability to King, but the facts clearly show that only King engaged in questionable actions and that only Brown was injured, so I assume that you meant to ask about King's potential liability to Brown, which I will discuss."

Similarly, if you need to fill a gap in a question to complete your analysis of an issue that otherwise is obviously raised by the facts, state your assumption about the omitted fact. The best assumption usually is that a special or unusual event did not occur if the facts omit any mention of that topic: "The facts do not state when Able received Baker's mailed notice of revocation, which is essential to the analysis of effective acceptance. I will assume, however, that it was neither sent by expedited service nor delayed in the mail and thus arrived in the normal course of mail delivery, which I assume would be the afternoon of December 17."

2. Do Not Lightly Alter the Facts of an Exam

Unless the exam contains an obvious error or an omission that is critical to your analysis of an issue that is otherwise clearly raised by the facts, you should be very wary of stating assumptions that supplement or vary the facts of an essay question. You must suppress any desire to change an exam question simply because you would prefer to respond to a different set of facts.

Thus, you should begin with a strong assumption that your professors mean what they say and that they are expecting you to analyze the question as it is written. If you do so and the question turns out to contain a mistake, your professor likely will give you as much credit as possible for analyzing the problem on the professor's mistaken facts, even if they do not support as rich a discussion as would be possible under the facts intended by the professor.

III. WRITING THE ANSWER

A. Production Rather Than Perfection

If you have prepared an outline of your answer, writing or typing the answer should be a fairly mechanical process. Your task is simply to express in full sentences the ideas that are represented in your examination outline, taking care to cover all the elements of a complete answer for each issue and subissue: issue, rule of law, application of law to facts, and conclusion (as discussed more fully in the next chapter). Your outline provides a guide that will keep you on track even when you momentarily lose sight of the main issues because of nervousness or temporary devotion to the details of a subissue.

Because of the intense time pressures of most in-class essay examinations, law professors do not expect polished writing or perfect organization, and you should not spend an inordinate amount of time thinking about the best possible way to express your ideas. Nonetheless, you will have an advantage if you have worked conscientiously in your Legal Writing class to develop skills of organization and clear, concise writing. You will score more points by clearly and efficiently expressing many relevant ideas and logical links than will students whose verbose and repetitious prose expresses fewer ideas in the same space or whose writing is so unclear or disorganized that the professor simply cannot understand it.

Beyond that, if the professor assigns raw points to relevant statements of law and fact, he or she might award points for such statements even if they are presented in a slightly disorganized manner, so long as the professor can find and understand them. Some professors, however, prefer to simply read an essay exam answer all the way through and then assign a grade based on their general assessment of the entire answer. Professors who use this approach to grading likely will end up assigning a higher score to an answer that is well written and logically organized than to an answer that includes precisely the same substance but is expressed in a sloppy or disorganized manner. If you have professors who use this latter approach to grading, you will derive great benefits from skills that you developed in your Legal Writing course and while outlining your other courses, and from the planning reflected in the minute or so that you devoted to outlining your exam answer on scratch paper.

If you run out of time, and are unable to complete your analysis in full prose, you should use your last few minutes to outline the remainder of your response in your examination answer booklet, even if your outline consists of no more than words or phrases to represent rules and relevant facts. Just as the host of a dinner party will prefer that you prepare all three tables in at least rudimentary fashion, most professors will give more points for a concise treatment of all the remaining ideas or issues than for a fuller development of only one of several remaining issues.

To save time, avoid restating lengthy legal rules that are relevant to more than one issue or question in an exam. Your professor will give you credit for knowing that the rule is relevant to both issues but almost certainly will not give you the same number of points twice for writing out the content of the rule twice. When the rule becomes relevant a second time, simply refer back to your earlier statement of the rule and move on to more fruitful targets for scoring points.

B. Express All the Links in Your Chain of Logic

The IRAC formulation is designed to remind you of all the elements of a full deductive argument. Do not fall into the trap of allowing one of the links in your chain of logic to sit perfectly clearly in your head but never make it onto paper. If this sounds trivial to you, let me warn you that it happens all the time. I have seen (1) analyses that were implicitly based on legal rules that test takers almost certainly knew but did not write down, (2) general factual conclusions, rather than references to specific facts at the evidentiary level, and (3) statements of the rules sitting alongside analyses of facts without any effort to tie the two together to show that the facts arguably satisfied or violated a particular rule.

When you write your answer, fill in the logical gaps; express the connections that are in your mind, waiting to leap onto the paper. The best way to do this is to assume that you are trying to educate someone who knows nothing about the problem and is skeptical of your arguments. The grader, who in fact knows all about the question and the model answer, is poised with a pen, ready to give you credit for every link in your chain of logic that you express, but is unable to give credit when you leave points unexpressed, even if he or she might infer from your discussion that you must know the point that you left sitting in your head rather than written on the paper.

C. Depth of Analysis

When researching the kind of essay exam answer that each of your professors prefers, among other things you should determine the extent to which your professor expects and rewards citations or other references to particular cases, statutes, or influential summaries of the common law, known as *Restatements* of law. When preparing an office memorandum for your Legal Writing class, you will carefully cite to cases and statutes, sometimes quote passages from them, synthesize cases to derive rules from them, and analogize and distinguish previous cases from the facts of the dispute before you. However, you will spend weeks researching, analyzing, and writing about a couple of issues in an office memorandum.

In contrast, your professor will test you on a course full of issues within the space of only a few hours. He or she can cover numerous issues with multiple-choice questions, thus relieving the essay questions of the burden of covering the entire course. Even, then, however, it would be impossible for you to address multiple issues in a three-hour essay examination with the same depth and formality expected of you in a good office memorandum.

The extent to which your essay answer should deviate from the in-depth discussion and citation to authority of an office memo can vary considerably between courses, so I describe a range and provide some examples and essay answers on various points of the spectrum. After setting forth a sample office memorandum on a single issue, I show how an essay answer can follow a structure similar to the discussion section of the office memo, but with varying degrees of departure from the memo's depth of analysis.

1. Sample Office Memorandum

Imagine that an attorney from the fictitious state of Calzona drafted the following office memorandum using only authority from the Calzona Supreme Court. The memo discusses a requirement for contract formation, known as *consideration*, which can be satisfied by an exchange of promises between parties—but only if their statements really commit them in ways consistent with the concept of a binding promise.

2. Sample Exam Answers on Same Issue

The following three sample exam answers address the same issue as that just discussed in the sample office memo. Although they do so with different depths of analysis, they share some general characteristics regarding the way they compare to the office memo.

First, the exam question will set forth the facts of your question, so you will simply waste time if you rewrite them at the beginning of your exam answer in the fashion of an office memo. Instead, you will state and analyze the facts relevant to each issue when you apply legal rules to your facts. Moreover, although you will identify each issue before you discuss it in an essay answer, and although your professor will give you credit for taking a stand and stating some reasonable conclusion at the end of your

MEMORANDUM

TO: Susan Elias
FROM: James Nelson
RE: Enforceability of Julie Week's Promise to Act as Guarantor
         for Her Cousin's Loan Obligation; File 11-127
DATE: July 27, 2013

I. ISSUE

By stating that he would refrain from demanding payment from Borrower on a loan obligation until he "needs the money," did Lender state a promise that provided consideration for Guarantor's promise to pay the obligation in the event that Borrower failed to pay on demand?

II. BRIEF ANSWER

Probably yes. Although the Lender's promise arguably is illusory, it probably satisfies the consideration requirement by committing the Lender to a performance, subject only to economic events not entirely within the Lender's control.

III. FACTS

One of our regular business clients, Julie Week (Guarantor), asserted the following facts in an interview.

On December 15, 2012, Guarantor's cousin, Don Caslin (Borrower), purchased two rare antique automobiles from a private owner, Thomas Beatty (Lender), for a total of $200,000. In a self-financing arrangement, Borrower paid $80,000 on delivery and agreed in writing to pay the remainder of the purchase price in 12 monthly installments of $10,000 each, beginning January 1, 2013.

From January to April 2013, Borrower paid Lender a total of $40,000 in monthly installments. In late April, however, Borrower suffered unusual losses in his private business, and he failed to pay the installments due on May 1 and June 1. After Lender threatened to sue for the return of the automobiles, Guarantor and Lender entered into a written agreement (the Guarantee Agreement) designed to give Borrower time to recover from his temporary financial difficulties. Dated June 6, 2013, the Guarantee Agreement refers to the agreement between Lender and Borrower as the

"CREDIT/SALE AGREEMENT," and it contains the following statement of mutual obligations:

1. LENDER will refrain from asserting his claim against BORROWER and from demanding payment on the CREDIT/SALE AGREEMENT until LENDER needs the money.
2. In the event that BORROWER fails to pay all amounts due under the CREDIT/SALE AGREEMENT upon demand by LENDER, GUARANTOR will pay those amounts immediately and will pay further installments as they become due under the CREDIT/SALE AGREEMENT.

On July 1, 2013, Lender demanded payment from Buyer of sums due from May through July, but Borrower explained that he could not yet pay anything. On July 5, 2013, Lender demanded immediate payment of $30,000 from Guarantor; he also stated that he expects either Borrower or Guarantor to pay the remaining five installments as they become due on the first of each month. Borrower states that he will not be able to make further payments for at least the remainder of this year, and Guarantor hopes to avoid responsibility for the debt.

We do not yet have any evidence that Lender engaged in fraud during formation of the Guarantee Agreement or that he lacked a genuine "need" for the money in early July. You have asked me to analyze the question whether the Guarantee Contract is unenforceable on its face for lack of consideration.

IV. DISCUSSION

Lender's promise to refrain from asserting his claim and demanding payment until he "needs the money" arguably is illusory. If so, Guarantor's promise is not supported by consideration and is unenforceable.

An enforceable contract requires consideration in the form of a bargained-for exchange in which a promisor exchanges his own promise for a return promise or performance. *Smith v. Newman*, 161 Calz. 443, 447, 667 P.2d 81, 85 (1984). The exchange can satisfy the consideration requirement even if one party's promise runs solely to the benefit of a third party rather than to the other party to the contract. *Id.* The requirement of an exchange, however, is not satisfied if one party gives only an illusory promise, which does not commit the promisor to any future performance. *Atco Corp. v. Johnson*, 155 Calz. 1211, 627 P.2d 781 (1980).

In *Atco Corp.*, the manager of an automobile repair shop purportedly promised to delay asserting a claim against the owner of an automobile for $900 in repairs. Specifically, he promised to forbear from asserting the claim "until I want the money." In exchange, a friend of the owner promised to act as guarantor of the owner's obligation. *Id.* at 1212, 627 P.2d at 782. The word "want" stated no legal commitment because it permitted the manager at his own discretion to refuse to perform any forbearance at all. Because the manager incurred no obligation, the guarantor's promise was gratuitous and unenforceable. *See id.* at 1213-14, 627 P.2d at 783-84.

On the other hand, even if a promise leaves open the possibility that the promisor will escape obligation, the promise is valid if the promisor does not have complete control over the events on which the promisor's obligation is conditioned. *Bonnie v. DeLaney*, 158 Calz. 212, 645 P.2d 887 (1982). In *Bonnie*, an agreement for the sale of a house provided that the buyer could cancel the agreement if the buyer "cannot qualify for a 30-year mortgage loan for 90% of the sales price" with any of several banks listed in the agreement. *Id.* at 213, 645 P.2d at 888. In enforcing the agreement against the seller, the court distinguished *Atco Corp.* on the ground that the word "cannot" referred to the buyer's ability to obtain a loan rather than to his desire. Because his ability to obtain a loan was partly controlled by events and decisions outside his control, the promises in the sale agreement were nonillusory and binding. *Id.* at 214-15, 645 P.2d at 889-90.

Despite the superficial similarity of guarantee agreements in both our case and *Atco. Corp.*, our client's case probably is more nearly analogous to *Bonnie*. Lender's promise to forbear until he "needs" the money appears to condition the length of his forbearance on financial events that are at least partly outside his control: As long as his income and expenses create no need for the money, Lender has a commitment to forbear from demanding payment.

To convince a court to draw an analogy to *Atco Corp.* rather than to *Bonnie*, we could argue that the word "need" refers to a subjective per-ception of deprivation that is inseparable from one's desires. Lender arguably can control his financial needs through his personal spending decisions, subject only to his own discretion.

Unfortunately for Guarantor, the analogy to *Bonnie* is stronger because financial need is normally viewed as a matter that is controlled at least partly by external factors. Lender's promise probably is not illusory.

V. CONCLUSION

The promises stated in the Guarantee Agreement appear to satisfy the consideration requirement, because Lender assumed a legal obliga-tion by promising to refrain from asserting his claim and demanding payment until he "needs" the money. Unless we discover other serious defects in the Guarantee Agreement or Lender's performance of it, Guarantor appears to be obligated to pay, and her defenses will not be worth litigating. We should urge Guarantor to settle Lender's claim, and we should try to persuade Borrower to indemnify Guarantor and to assume responsibility for further payments, even if he must sell the cars or other property to generate funds.

discussion of that issue, you normally will not earn extra points by stating all of the issues and brief answers together in a formal statement at the beginning of your answer, as in an office memo.

Thus, the counterpart to your essay exam answer is the discussion section of the office memo, where you normally use the IRAC approach to analyze each issue and present arguments for both sides. Because of time constraints, your essay answer will be less formal than the discussion section of an office memorandum, to varying degrees, as illustrated by the following three sample answers.

a. In-Depth Answer

Some professors want to see exam answers that identify by name cases studied in class and that discuss how those cases relate to the dispute presented in the exam question. This is perhaps most likely in a course that addresses issues governed by a few landmark decisions of the U.S. Supreme Court that were discussed in great depth in class. It is much less likely in a course on Contracts, in which a large number of state court decisions develop and apply numerous rules. Let's imagine, however, that a professor in a Contracts course gives a higher score to exam answers that name cases studied in the course and compare those cases to the dispute raised in the essay exam question, and let's suppose that the professor gives you sufficient time to prepare such an answer.

You can assume that an essay exam question in this professor's course begins with the second sentence of the statement of facts in the preceding sample office memorandum, and that it substitutes the following for the final sentence of the fact statement: "Fully discuss whether the Guarantee Contract is unenforceable on its face for lack of consideration." Because the professor has identified a single issue for you to discuss, and assuming that the exam allows a generous allotment of time to answer this question, you might prepare a fairly in-depth response such as the following. In this and the following examples, the bold italicized labels at the margin are for your benefit and probably should not appear on the exam itself, lest your professor be distracted by the overt reference to the elements of IRAC.

Issue:	Q1—Consideration (Illusory Promise)
Rule:	An enforceable contract requires a bargained-for exchange in which a promisor exchanges his own promise for a return promise or performance. The requirement of an exchange is not satisfied if one party gives only an illusory promise, which does not commit the promisor to any future performance.
	For example, the *Atco* case in our casebook found no consideration in a repair shop manager's statement that he would delay asserting a claim for money owed "until I want the money."

The word "want" stated no legal commitment because it permitted the manager at his own discretion to refuse to perform any forbearance at all. Thus, this statement was not a promise that could be exchanged for the other party's promise to guarantee the debt.

Still, even if a promise leaves open the possibility that the promisor will escape obligation, the promise is valid if the promisor does not have complete control over the events on which the promisor's obligation is conditioned. In *Bonnie v. DeLaney*, the buyer of a house had the right to cancel the purchase agreement if the buyer "cannot qualify" for a particular kind of loan. The buyer's promise to buy was binding because the word "cannot" referred to the buyer's ability to obtain a loan rather than to his desire, and his ability to obtain a loan was partly controlled by events and decisions outside his control.

Application to facts: The facts of our question arguably fall between those of *Atco* and *Bonnie*. Lender can argue that his promise to forbear until he "needs" the money, similar to the condition of "cannot qualify" in *Bonnie*, appears to condition the length of his forbearance on financial events that are at least partly outside his control: As long as his income and expenses create no need for the money, Lender has a commitment to forbear from demanding payment. Accordingly, Lender's promise would provide consideration for Guarantor's promise. Guarantor, however, can argue that the word "need" is more like the condition based on "want" in *Atco*. It refers to a subjective perception of deprivation that is inseparable from one's desires. Lender arguably can control his financial needs through his personal spending decisions, subject only to his own discretion.

Conclusion: On balance I conclude . . . .

You will notice that this essay exam answer does not set forth the full citation to relevant case precedent, but it does refer to cases by name, describe their facts, and attempt to draw analogies between them and the dispute in the exam question. Such an answer goes a long way toward displaying the kinds of skills that students will apply in practice, so an exam question that solicits such an analysis deserves our praise. It would also, however, be highly unusual, except perhaps in a take-home exam. In a typical in-class essay exam, your professor will attempt to cover so many issues in such a short period of time that he or she simply cannot expect an in-depth analysis such as the example above. The next example, therefore, is a better representation of the kind of analysis that would normally be feasible under examination conditions.

b. Full IRAC with Moderate Depth of Analysis

More typically, an essay exam question that identified a single issue for discussion would be a "warm-up" question to which relatively little time was allotted. Alternatively, the consideration issue discussed in the previous illustrations would be one of two or more issues that you would be expected to identify and discuss within a time period that would not permit the kind of in-depth case analysis set forth in the previous sample answer.

Instead, time pressure likely would dictate an answer that summarizes the legal rules in the manner in which you stated them in your course outline. True, you derived those rules from your analyses and syntheses of cases, and illustrating the rules with the holdings of cases helps you understand how the rules might apply to new facts; however, you likely will not have time to refer to the specific cases from which you derived the rules. Thus, assuming that the exam question raised three issues, your essay answer to the consideration issue might look like the following:

Issue: Offer and Acceptance:
        . . .

Issue: Consideration—Illusory Promise:
        This lender's promise to refrain from asserting his claim and demanding payment until he "needs the money" arguably is illusory, thus creating doubt whether the guarantor's promise is enforceable.

Rule: An enforceable contract requires a bargained-for exchange in which a promisor exchanges his own promise for a return promise or performance. This requirement is not satisfied if one party gives only an illusory promise, which does not commit the promisor to any performance, but leaves performance entirely within her discretion. Even if a promise leaves open the possibility that the promisor will escape obligation, however, the promise is valid if the promisor does not have complete control over the events on which the promisor's obligation is conditioned.

Application: Lender's promise to forbear until he "needs" the money arguably conditions the length of his forbearance on financial events that are at least partly outside his control: As long as his income and expenses created no need for the money, Lender had a commitment to forbear from demanding payment, thus providing consideration for the guarantor's promise.
        In response, Guarantor could argue that the word "need" refers to a subjective perception of deprivation that is inseparable from one's desires, which are subject to the promisor's unfettered

discretion. Lender arguably could create financial "needs" entirely at his own discretion simply by spending more money.

Conclusion:	On balance, I conclude . . . .
Issue:	Quasi-Contract:
	. . .

This sample answer is complete and sophisticated, and its fact analysis is essentially the same as that in the first example. It is a bit more streamlined in its statement of the legal rule, however, because it does not analyze or even refer to case precedent. To invoke the metaphor raised earlier in this chapter, it represents a successful setting of all three tables for the dinner party, albeit not in the grand fashion of an answer that cited and analyzed case precedent.

c. Hurried Analysis in an "Issue-Spotting" Exam

Some professors try to cover so many issues in such a short time that you will not have sufficient time to develop your discussion in a deliberate fashion. Instead, if your research shows that this professor gives the highest scores to those students who spot all the issues and discuss each of them to the extent possible within time limits, you should identify every issue that you can, and provide an abbreviated discussion of the law and facts, as permitted by time pressures. Assuming that the question raised numerous issues without allowing a generous amount of time, your exam answer might look like the following:

Issue:	Offer and Acceptance:
Subissue:	Lapse:
	. . .
Subissue:	Mirror-Image Rule:
	. . .
Issue:	Consideration—Illusory Promise:
Rule and factual argument:	The consideration requirement is not satisfied if one party gives only an illusory promise, which does not commit the promisor to any future performance, but leaves performance entirely to his discretion. Guarantor's promise might be illusory because he can escape obligation to forbear simply by "needing" the money, which he arguably can control simply by spending money and thus creating financial needs.

More rule and factual counter argument:	However, the promise is valid if the promisor does not have complete control over the events on which the promisor's obligation is conditioned. And "needs" likely would be interpreted to depend on financial events that are at least partly outside Lender's control. Thus, Lender's promise likely is binding, providing consideration for Guarantor's promise.
Issue:	Parol Evidence Rule: . . .
Issue:	Penalty Clause Against Public Policy: . . .

Indeed, if you were really pressed for time, you might be forced to sacrifice a full IRAC format, by focusing on factual arguments and referring to legal rules only implicitly:

Consideration—Illusory Promise:

Lender's "promise" might be illusory because he is not bound to perform if he "needs" the money, which arguably is entirely within his control based on his discretionary spending decisions. On the other hand, he probably is bound, thus providing consideration for Guarantor's promise, because his "needs" would depend on financial events partly outside Lender's control.

This last example is a little like sacrificing the tablecloths in a successful effort to set up all the tables with chairs and silverware: It is not particularly pretty, but everyone gets a seat at the table, and it even argues both sides of the question.

IV. THE NEXT STEP

At this point you have gained considerable knowledge about general exam technique: Do not stop now. Move to the next chapter to learn more about traditional fact-based essay exams that solicit arguments for both sides of the dispute.

CHAPTER 10

Fact-Based Essay Questions with Uncertain Answers

Most essay examinations position the reader as a neutral observer and ask for a balanced analysis of a problem with a direction such as, "Discuss the claims and defenses that the parties may reasonably assert." The call of the question might also instruct you to "discuss legal or factual arguments for both sides, whenever possible." Even in the absence of such a specific instruction to argue both sides, however, you might conclude that the question invites competing arguments on the basis of other factors. For example, you might draw this inference from your professor's previous exams and model answers, from his or her comments in class about the upcoming exam, or from facts in the exam question that obviously support arguments for both sides.

This chapter discusses the substantive components of your answer to such an essay question. The next chapter addresses other kinds of essay questions, including those that require an explanation of how and why legal rules apply facts to reach a particular conclusion, or that ask for policy analysis outside the context of a particular fact pattern.

I. GENERAL FORMAT

As introduced earlier in this book, an answer to an essay examination and the discussion section of an office memorandum typically share a general structure associated with the acronym IRAC: After identifying the *issue*, you should summarize the applicable legal *rule* or rules, *apply* the rule to the relevant facts to determine whether the facts satisfy the legal rule, and state a reasonable *conclusion*. These elements correspond to the pattern of deductive reasoning and thus are apt to appear as a complete and well-organized analysis when presented in that order.

You should maintain flexibility, however, to adapt your format in any way that allows you to effectively answer the question in a fluid, logically organized style. Moreover, even when the IRAC formulation represents the perfect way to lay out your analysis, remember that this acronym serves only as a handy device for recalling the components of a full argument. Although this book sometimes names each element of the IRAC format, such as "Rule," alongside a sample essay answer, it does so only to help you learn and identify the elements of a complete analysis. You should avoid making such explicit reference to the elements of IRAC in your own essay exam answers, because such an overly conspicuous roadmap will strike some professors as excessively mechanical. Instead, use a section heading or a strong topic sentence, or both, to identify an issue, and then use good paragraphing to signal your progression from one element to another, such as from rule to fact application.

As introduced in Chapter 9, some of the more formal components of other legal documents are notably missing from a good exam answer. For example, professors normally do not require you to formally state all the issues and conclusions at or near the beginning of your answer, as you would in an office memorandum or in some briefs. Even more important, you should never waste time drafting an introduction that separately restates all the facts of the problem. After all, a traditional essay question largely consists of a statement of facts, so there is no need for you to repeat that statement at the beginning of your answer. I suspect that some students do this in their exam answers because they are nervous and find that restating the facts helps them loosen up. If my speculation is correct, I recommend that they redirect that nervous energy to an outline of the analysis on scratch paper.

Of course, you will eventually address the facts in a special way: After identifying an issue and stating the applicable rule, you will then discuss whether the facts relevant to that issue satisfy the rule. Accordingly, your professor will test your ability to analyze groups of relevant facts in the context of specific issues, but not your ability to restate all the facts at the outset.

II. ELEMENTS OF THE ANSWER

A. Issues

Generally speaking, an issue is a reasonably debatable question about the content of the law, or about the application of law to facts. Thus, if an exam question raises a question over which two attorneys could reasonably argue in court, it presents an issue that warrants full discussion in IRAC form.

The next chapter addresses exam questions that raise issues with certain answers but that nonetheless are complicated, so that the examiner is interested in your ability to explain how and why the complex law applies to the facts in order to reach a certain conclusion. If part of the exam question refers to a matter that is both well established in the law and is simply resolved, however, then it does not raise an issue over which a judge would invite argument in court; that part of the exam simply refers to a matter for which you could state a certain legal conclusion with only brief explanation. Perhaps that conclusion is worth mentioning because it establishes a premise that helps to set up other issues that warrant fuller discussion; however, it does not itself raise a debatable "issue" that requires extended analysis.

1. Identifying Issues

Occasionally, a professor will identify examination issues by asking you to respond to specific questions or directions, such as the following:

- Did Seller make an offer to Buyer?
- How would the doctrine of pure comparative negligence apply to these facts?
- Discuss whether Ida has acquired rights through adverse possession of the property.

More commonly, the exam problem will end with a very general question about the rights and obligations of the party, and it will require you to identify the relevant issues. To identify the issues, you must apply the skills and knowledge that you have acquired from briefing cases and outlining course material throughout the semester. By briefing countless cases, you learn to sift through complicated fact patterns and recognize the kinds of facts that courts deemed to have legal significance. Moreover, by briefing and synthesizing cases and by outlining the course material, you arm yourself with a general knowledge of relevant legal rules and policies. With this preparation, and with your mastery of the facts of the exam problem, you can determine what claims and defenses the parties can reasonably assert and which elements of those claims and defenses are placed in doubt.

a. An Example from a Nonlegal Context

To illustrate this point with a simple nonlegal example, let's review the Grocer's Problem in Chapter 4. You know from statements by the grocer and from previous cases that the grocer will place produce in the window display case if—like the round, red, shiny apples of the first case—they would tend to attract pedestrians into the store. Otherwise—as in the second case of the unwashed carrots—the produce goes in the interior of the store, in a place convenient to shoppers who had already intended to enter and shop.

A question about proper placement might be raised by facts that describe some new produce being delivered to the store. If the new delivery is a crate of apples identical to those in the first case, the answer appears to be fairly certain, because the grocer has previously decided that apples like those should be placed in the window display case. Those facts do not give you much to debate, so they do not raise an issue worth discussing fully. Your professor is not likely to give you such a question, though, because he or she is interested in testing your ability to analyze facts you have not discussed in class, and not just your memory of the outcome of a previous case.

Now, if the newly delivered produce is a crate of large, shiny, red bell peppers, you should be uncertain of the proper location of the peppers. You can imagine two reasonable store employees differing about whether the peppers were more clearly analogous to the apples or to the carrots of the previous cases. If you can construct plausible arguments supporting each of these competing positions, you have a substantial issue about the proper placement of the peppers, one worth discussing fully.

b. An Example from the Common Law of Burglary

For an example in a legal context, suppose that an exam problem asks you to assume that the relevant jurisdiction has retained the common law definition of burglary. Part of the problem describes Robert Glass opening the unlocked door of the cab of a van and reaching inside to steal a laptop computer lying on the driver's seat. The owner of the van, Leona Rosal, is sleeping in the back of the van while on a road trip, with curtains drawn between her and the cab of the van. The event takes place at 5:30 A.M., when a faint light in the sky just prior to sunrise enables Glass to see the outlines of the portable computer. The problem also asks you to assume that theft of the portable computer would constitute felony larceny in the jurisdiction.

You know from your studies that the common law crime of burglary requires proof of the breaking and entering of a dwelling of another at night with the intent to commit a felony. Armed with this knowledge, you can see that the facts provide a nonfrivolous basis for prosecuting Robert Glass for common law burglary. For example, Glass's opening the cab door and reaching into the van for the purpose of stealing the laptop computer almost certainly constitute "breaking and entering" with an "intent to commit a felony." These elements of the crime probably do not raise issues warranting substantial discussion. At most, you might briefly explain that the element of breaking does not require force and therefore could be accomplished by opening an unlocked door, but that is not a debatable matter that requires extended discussion.

Other elements of the crime, however, are in greater doubt. Even though Leona had drawn her curtains to permit her to sleep late, and although the sun had not yet risen, the event only arguably takes place "during the night" because faint predawn light has increased visibility sufficiently for Glass to see the outlines of the laptop computer. Additionally, the van might be unlike the more conventional houses that satisfied the "dwelling" requirement in the common law cases that you have studied. Although Leona is temporarily using the van as sleeping quarters, the van is arguably primarily a means of transportation, and the cab—where the burglary took place—is physically separated from the sleeping quarters. Thus, whether Glass committed a burglary is subject to some debate and is a general issue in the problem.

Moreover, each element of the crime that is in doubt forms the basis of a subissue. For example, under the heading "During the Night," you would summarize the rules and policies associated with this element of burglary, and then apply them to the facts, arguing both sides. Similarly, under the heading "Dwelling," you would summarize the rules and policies that you had learned about this element and apply them to the facts. Because you can reasonably argue both sides of these topics, whether the event took place during the night and whether Leona's van is a dwelling for purposes of common law burglary are subissues warranting discussion.

2. Scope of Analysis

Because the process of identifying issues requires you to exercise judgment, you can never determine with complete certainty which questions your professor thinks are sufficiently clearly raised by the facts to warrant discussion. Moreover, some professors directly examine your ability to identify as many issues as possible, including those related to novel or particularly creative legal theories. When in doubt, therefore, you should first discuss the issues that are clearly raised by the facts and then use any remaining time to identify and at least briefly discuss even marginal issues. If the professor expects some discussion of a marginal issue, you will earn valuable points for even a brief discussion. On the other hand, if the professor disagrees that a particular matter warrants analysis, you will have minimized the lost time by keeping the discussion brief.

3. Expressing Your Identification of Issues

You need not state each of the issues and subissues of an examination problem in polished detail. However, your essay answer should leave no doubt about which issue you are analyzing in any passage in the answer. To guide your reader through your analysis, you can use the same techniques that help convey organization to the reader in the discussion section of an office memorandum. Be certain to discuss each issue separately, completing one issue or subissue before beginning your discussion of the next one.

To provide a clear roadmap to your reader, precede your discussion of a major issue with a section heading that generally identifies the issue, such as "Consideration," "Burglary," "Negligence," or "Defense:

Assumption of the Risk." Unless the question raises the possibility of claims of only one party against one other, section headings also should identify which party is bringing a claim against which other party in each section.

For example, an exam question might raise issues about various tort claims between various pairings of three parties: Smith, Jones, and King. A student might display the general organization of his or her answer with section headings such as the following:

> Smith v. Jones
>> Battery
>> . . .
>> Infliction of Emotional Distress
>> . . .
>
> Smith v. King
>> Negligence
>> . . .
>> Vicarious Liability
>> . . .
>
> Jones v. Smith
>> Defamation
>> . . .

In some cases, you might wish to illuminate the issue that is denoted by a section heading by using an introductory sentence or two to refer briefly to a potential argument of one of the parties, facts that raise the issue, or a preliminary legal conclusion that sets up the issue. For example, immediately under "Smith v. King, Negligence" in the preceding example, you might provide this orientation: "Smith may claim that King negligently hired Jones, making King liable for Smith's injuries at Jones's hands." Alternatively, either beneath the heading or in place of it, you could simply state this issue in question form: "Is King liable to Smith for negligently hiring Jones?" Although a fuller, more precise, more fact-specific statement of the issue might be appropriate for an office memorandum or a brief, you will not have time for such perfection in an essay exam. Your goal in an exam is to make clear at every step which issue you are discussing, and you frequently can achieve that goal with a section heading or a concise statement of the issue.

If your analysis of an issue is lengthy or complex, you might want to use subsection headings to identify your discussions of subissues, with or without section numbers and letters.

> Smith v. Jones
>> *Intentional Infliction of Emotional Distress*

> [overview of elements of claim]
> Extreme and Outrageous Conduct—
> . . .
> Intent or Recklessness—
> . . .
> Severe Emotional Distress—
> . . .
> Causation—
> . . .

In simpler cases, however, subtler guides to the reader often will be sufficient to identify subissues. You can separate your discussions of distinct subissues into separate paragraphs, and you can use a topic sentence to identify the subissue addressed in each paragraph, in the same breath in which you begin to state the rule.

> Intentional Infliction of Emotional Distress:
> [overview of elements of claim]
> "Extreme and outrageous" conduct is limited to . . . . Viewed in isolation, Principal Jones's method of questioning Schoolboy Smith about illegal drugs . . . .
> Reckless disregard for the risk of causing severe distress can be established through . . . . In this case, Principal Jones was aware . . . .
> Severe emotional distress means more than . . . .

In response to a complex essay question that raises multiple issues, you might help orient the reader by beginning your response with an introductory sentence or two that briefly identifies all the major issues that you plan to discuss. However, you should not choose that path if it would take more than a few moments of your precious time, or if it would result in a lengthy introduction that makes the subsequent discussion sound redundant.

B. Legal Rule

1. Presentation of Legal Rules

At the broadest level, the statement of a legal rule can consist of a summary of the elements of a claim that a party in the examination problem might reasonably pursue.

> Intentional Infliction of Emotional Distress:
> Principal Jones may be liable to Schoolboy Smith for intentional infliction of emotional distress if he engaged in extreme and outrageous conduct that caused Smith severe emotional distress, and if Jones either intended to

cause such distress or recklessly disregarded the near certainty of causing such distress.

If you divide the discussion of this claim into subsections or paragraphs to address separate subissues, you might state a subrule in the form of a definition or other illumination of one of the elements of the claim.

"Extreme and outrageous" conduct is limited to shocking conduct that is beyond all possible bounds of decency. The defendant's conduct is more likely to satisfy this standard if he occupies a position of power or authority over the plaintiff.

Some examination problems might raise questions or debates about choice of law or the precise formulation of the applicable rule. For example, a problem in a contracts examination might raise the question of whether the judicially developed common law or the legislatively enacted Uniform Commercial Code applies to a transaction. Other examination problems might raise questions about the choice between traditional rules and progressive trends, or between majority rules and minority approaches. If you have time to discuss such problems, you should consider briefly discussing each of the competing rules. Then, in the fact analysis that follows, you can discuss the likelihood of success of a claim or defense under each legal rule.

Alternatively, as in the following example, you can present one of the competing rules and apply it to the facts, before presenting the other rule and applying it to the facts in its own IRAC.

Under the traditional majority rule, a promise is not supported by consideration unless it was exchanged for the other party's promise or performance with reciprocal inducement. This means that each party is induced to give his own promise or performance by the prospect of receiving the other party's promise or performance. Reciprocal inducement thus is lacking if a promise is given in recognition of a past act, because the past act could not have been induced by a promise that does not yet exist.

In this case, McGee's promise almost certainly is gratuitous and thus unenforceable under the traditional majority rule, because Weber and McGee did not have an opportunity to exchange promises before Weber acted to save McGee's home, belongings, and pets from certain destruction by the fire. Weber might invite a court to infer such a bargain from the general discussion between McGee and Weber before McGee left for vacation, because . . . However, ...

Under a modern trend adopted by some courts, on the other hand, McGee's promise might be enforceable—even in the absence of an exchange of promises—if it was given in recognition of a moral obligation to compensate Weber for some past act. Such a moral obligation may arise if the promisee had provided an extraordinary benefit to the promisor, such as saving the promisor from death or serious injury, particularly if the promisee unavoidably suffered serious injury in doing so.

McGee may argue that no moral obligation arose, because the benefit provided by Weber's past act was not one of directly preserving the personal health or life of McGee, who was out of town at the time of the fire. Nonetheless, McGee acknowledged that he promised to pay Weber $50,000 in recognition for his heroics. Moreover, he admitted that he would have gone crazy had he lost his pets and personal effects, suggesting that Weber's act must have helped preserve McGee's emotional health.

The case for moral obligation is also weakened by the fact that Weber did not sustain any permanent injuries in putting out the fire. On the other hand, Weber's smoke inhalation did require treatment at the hospital emergency room and caused him considerable pain and trauma . . . .

Finally, you can earn extra points if you find an opportunity to demonstrate that you understand the purpose or policy underlying or supporting a rule. In the preceding illustration, for example, you might mention that the trend to recognize moral obligation as a basis for enforcing a promise enables courts to achieve a just result in exceptional cases, but that the traditional rule promotes certainty and predictability by rejecting amorphous exceptions to its test for enforceable exchanges.

For another example, recall the burglary of the van discussed earlier in this chapter. If your discussion of the rule mentioned that this common law crime especially singled out intrusions during the night because victims were most vulnerable when they were sleeping and when the perpetrator is cloaked in darkness, then you might use that underlying purpose or policy to help you generate arguments in your fact analysis about whether the event in that case took place during the night. You might mention, for example, that most people are still sleeping at 5:30 A.M. and thus are still vulnerable to a degree that the early common law meant to address with its harsh penalties. For the defense, you could argue that the charge should be limited to larceny and should not include the serious charge of common law burglary, because the faint light just before sunrise made the suspect visible and perhaps even recognizable to someone who was sleeping lightly.

2. Depth and Formality of Analysis

When writing an office memorandum, you normally must discuss specific statutes and case law from a particular jurisdiction that apply to the dispute, and you must carefully cite the authority on which you rely. Moreover, you often will present the in-depth case analysis and synthesis from which you derive a legal rule.

In contrast, as illustrated with several examples in Chapter 9, most law school examinations will require you to discuss general legal principles that you must memorize for a closed-book examination. Additionally, you ordinarily will not have time to describe the process of synthesizing cases from which you have derived legal rules for your outlines. Instead, you can simply present the kind of concise statements of law that you have previously constructed for your outlines.

Moreover, unless your professor instructs otherwise, you ordinarily need not cite to case law in your discussion of legal rules in an examination answer. You might earn an extra point or two by identifying the names of particular cases that illustrate issues or rules, but that practice is productive only if you remember the case name quickly and accurately. The extra point or two is not worth a significant investment of time, and the possibility of losing points or precious time by naming an irrelevant case reduces the appeal of guessing.

Some professors' expectations might be greater, particularly if they give an open-book examination with adequate time for full discussion and especially if they provide extra time in a take-home examination. If you are allowed to bring the casebook or your notes into the examination, you can more easily identify the names of relevant cases and maybe even explain how two or more cases combine to contribute to the development of a legal principle. Still, this remains an exception to the general rule that references to case names are not necessary if you can otherwise state the legal rule clearly.

The presumption is the opposite for citations to applicable statutes. Unless your professor tells you otherwise, you should cite the section numbers of important statutes, like UCC § 2-207. Moreover, if the interpretation or application of a statutory word or phrase is in issue, you normally should quote the precise statutory language in question, particularly if you are allowed to take your statutory supplement into the examination room.

All of these recommendations, of course, are based on typical positions taken by law professors. As always, you should question your professors or look at past exams and model answers to determine the form in which each of your professors prefers statements of legal rules.

C. Fact Analysis: Application of Law to Facts

1. Presentation of Fact Analysis

In each section or subsection devoted to an issue or subissue, you should identify facts relevant to the issue and should briefly explain whether the facts satisfy the legal rule that you have just summarized. In most cases, you have identified a matter as an issue because the facts of the problem suggest uncertainty about whether a legal rule is satisfied. Therefore, you usually can find some facts that support each side of the dispute, and you should take care to argue both sides, as illustrated in the third paragraph of the following sample.

> Intentional Infliction of Emotional Distress:
>
> Principal Jones may be liable if he engaged in extreme and outrageous conduct, causing Schoolboy Smith to suffer severe emotional distress, and if Jones acted with the intent to cause such distress or with reckless disregard of the risk of such harm.
>
> *Extreme and Outrageous Conduct*—Conduct meets this standard if it would be shocking to a reasonable member of the community. It may more easily meet this standard if engaged in by a person with authority over the victim.
>
> Principal Jones's method of questioning Schoolboy Smith about illegal drugs probably was not "extreme and outrageous" in itself, because Jones "addressed Smith politely" and "never raised his voice." On the other hand, Jones was inherently intimidating to Smith, a 10-year-old child, because of Jones's status as an adult and the highest authority at the elementary school. Moreover, it was common knowledge in the school that Jones had sus-pended two other students that semester for forging false notes excusing absences. By asking Smith to empty his pockets and to reveal the contents of his desk and locker, Jones implicitly accused Smith of lying when Smith denied any involvement with illegal drugs. In light of Jones's position of authority, his request to search Smith may have been unusually shocking and intimidating, particularly because the request immediately followed Smith's sincere denials.
>
> On balance, I conclude . . . .

Did you notice the elements of IRAC in this sample answer? The first heading states the general issue and the opening paragraph states the general rule, governing the entire tort claim. The answer then launches into a separate IRAC to address a single element of the general rule. The subheading identifies that issue (the element of extreme and outra-geous conduct), and the paragraph immediately after the subheading states the subrule, in the form of a definition of "extreme and outrageous conduct." The next paragraph, the longest one in the passage, analyzes and argues the facts relevant to that subrule, and the final paragraph states a conclusion. If another element of the tort is in dispute, that can be ana-lyzed in a separate IRAC, with its own subheading.

2. Depth and Formality of Fact Analysis

In an office memorandum, you explore in depth the application of legal rules to facts by carefully comparing the facts and reasoning of previous cases to the facts of your own case. Through this process of analogizing and distinguishing precedent, you can thoroughly analyze the facts of your case to determine whether they satisfy the applicable legal rules.

In contrast, few professors will expect you to describe the facts of particular cases studied in class and to expressly analogize them to or distinguish them from the facts presented in an exam problem. If you have conscientiously briefed your cases throughout the semester, you will recall cases that help you to spot issues and to analyze the problem, and you might mentally draw direct factual distinctions and analogies. However, you will seldom have sufficient time to express those distinctions and analogies in thorough case analysis in your examination answer. Instead, you should directly explain how relevant facts support or undermine the application of a legal rule, as in the example in the previous subsection.

As with statements of legal rules, professors might have higher expectations if they give open-book exams or if the course is dominated by a manageable number of memorable cases. If you have mastered a relatively small number of important cases that define an area of law, you can feasibly refer to them by name and develop factual analogies and distinctions, even if you do not have access to your course materials during the examination. Again, it pays to ask your professor about such things or to form conclusions based on past exams and model answers.

D. The Conclusion

1. Taking a Position

This chapter addresses essay questions raising issues that do not have "correct" answers because of uncertainty in the law or in the application of the law to novel facts. On such issues, the professor expects you to argue both sides of the dispute and will not be concerned about which conclusion you believe is the strongest.

Nonetheless, just as your supervising attorney will expect you to reach conclusions, in the form of predictions, on even close questions in an office memorandum, most law professors will expect you to state a conclusion for each issue that you discuss in an examination answer. On close questions, you can hedge the conclusion with qualifying terms, such as "probably." In the following excerpt, the major issue of the claim of intentional infliction of emotional distress encompasses four subissues corresponding to the four elements of that tort. The discussion of each of those subissues ends with a subsidiary conclusion regarding that subissue, and the entire discussion ends with a more general conclusion about the entire claim.

> Intentional Infliction of Emotional Distress:
>   Principal Jones may be liable to Schoolboy Smith . . . .
>   *Extreme and Outrageous Conduct*:
>   [rule and fact analysis on this subissue]

In conclusion, Principal Jones's questioning and request to search constituted extreme and outrageous conduct.

Intent or Recklessness:
[rule and fact analysis on this subissue]
Although Principal Jones may not have intended to inflict severe emotional distress, he probably acted recklessly.

Severe Emotional Distress:
[rule and fact analysis on this subissue]
Smith's transitory fear probably did not amount to severe emotional distress.

Causation:
[rule and fact analysis on this subissue]
Any fear that Smith suffered over the incident was directly caused by Principal Jones's reckless actions.

Because Schoolboy Smith probably did not suffer extreme emotional distress, I conclude that Principal Jones is not liable for intentional infliction of emotional distress.

2. Comprehensive Conclusions

In an office memorandum, you should not only state conclusions at the end of your discussion of each issue and subissue, but also summarize all your major conclusions and express your recommendations in a separate conclusion section.

In contrast, few law professors will expect you to summarize all previous major conclusions in a general summary of conclusions at the end of your answer to an exam question. Such a consolidated restatement of conclusions will score few points in an exam unless it adds new information or enhances the clarity of the discussion that precedes it. In most cases, accordingly, you will benefit by using your last few minutes to look for additional issues or arguments that you might have missed rather than to summarize conclusions that you have already clearly communicated in your discussions of individual issues.

3. Do Not Cut Off Secondary Issues

If your professor has provided you with facts that invite discussion of an issue, do not fail to discuss that issue solely on the basis of your resolution of a close question on a logically prior issue. To take an obvious example, suppose that an exam question presents facts that raise interesting issues about (1) whether *A* and *B* formed a contract through offer and acceptance, (2) whether *A* breached the contract by failing to perform as agreed, and (3) whether *B* could recover damages for certain kinds of losses. If the first issue presented a close question on the facts, your professor likely would not care whether you concluded that the parties formed a contract or not, so long as you discussed the relevant law and the factual arguments for both sides.

Nonetheless, if you concluded that the parties did not form a contract, you should not then determine that it is unnecessary for you to discuss the issues of breach and remedies, particularly if the facts obviously raise those issues. Instead, after concluding that the parties failed to form a contract, you would state your assumption that a court might reach the opposite conclusion on that threshold issue, and address the remaining issues.

III. SAMPLE ESSAY QUESTIONS AND ANSWERS

A. A Nonlegal Example

So that you can focus solely on the form of a question and answer, let's begin with an example that does not require knowledge of complicated legal rules. Let's start with a statement of some rules in the nonlegal setting of parents placing limitations on their young child's activities in the house:

I. Overview: Debbie's parents try to restrict Debbie's activities to those that are beneficial to her health and that protect her parents' possessions from harm.

II. Dietary Rules: Debbie is permitted to eat sweets, but only at times that won't spoil her appetite for more healthful foods.
   A. Example: In *The Case of the Chocolate Ice Cream,* Debbie's parents gladly served her ice cream after dinner, because she had eaten all her vegetables.
   B. Example: In *The Case of the Hand in the Cookie Jar,* Debbie was not permitted to eat a cookie shortly before dinner, because it would ruin her appetite for dinner.

III. Rules about Toys: Debbie is permitted to play only with her own toys, and not in a way that will endanger her parents' possessions.
   A. Example: In *The Case of the Broken Vase,* Debbie was disciplined for breaking her parents' vase.
   B. Example: In *The Case of the Bouncing Ball,* Debbie was admonished for playing with her own rubber ball in a way that endangered her parents' possessions, such as the TV set and wine glasses.
   C. Example: In *The Case of the Mistreated Teddy Bear,* Debbie was permitted to play with her own teddy bear, even by throwing it onto the floor, apparently because this conduct did not harm any of her parents' possessions.

These rules might sound a little simple-minded, but they can result in a fairly sophisticated application of rules to facts. For example, section II of the following sample answer responds to novel facts by engaging in policy analysis to present an extension of the rule that was devised from earlier cases. Notice in the sample answer that each of the major issues is identified in each section heading, that each simple rule is identified in a single sentence at the beginning of each section, and that most of the answer consists of factual arguments.

Sample Essay Question

On Saturday morning, Debbie began coloring in her coloring book with a box of crayons. She soon expanded her artistic activity to drawing a multi-colored mural on one of the walls of her room. Displeased with the quality of her drawing, Debbie broke each of her 24 crayons in half and threw them into her wastebasket. Indeed, she was so displeased with her artistry that she decided to wash her drawing off the wall. To that end, Debbie opened the cupboard under the kitchen sink and took a bottle of liquid drain cleaner, which she thought was a form of soap but was in fact a toxic chemical capable of burning her eyes and skin. At that moment, Debbie's parents intercepted her and discovered each of her activities during the day. Fully discuss whether Debbie has violated any rules of her house.

Sample Essay Answer

I. Harm to Parents' Possessions

Debbie's parents permit her to use and even abuse her own toys, but they do not allow Debbie to harm their possessions.

Debbie did not harm her parents' property by drawing in her coloring book. And she probably did not harm their property by breaking her crayons, because those presumably were her own toys. However, Debbie almost certainly violated her parents' rules by drawing on her bedroom wall. Although the wall was in her room, her parents probably view it as part of their possessions, because they undoubtedly are responsible for maintaining it. Debbie did not physically break the surface of the wall as she might break a vase. However, a crayon drawing on the wall might require vigorous scrubbing or even repainting. Therefore, it probably represents actual harm to the wall.

Debbie has violated her parents' rule against harming their possessions.

II. Promotion of Debbie's Health and Protection of Parents' Possessions

In addition to prohibiting Debbie from harming their possessions, Debbie's parents forbid her to eat sweets if they will spoil her appetite for more healthful foods.

Debbie has not tried to eat sweets at an inappropriate time. However, she has endangered her health by carrying a dangerous chemical, the drain cleaner, with the intention of opening the bottle and using the chemical to clean her wall. The policy behind the dietary rule is apparently to help maintain Debbie's health. Therefore, Debbie's parents likely would disapprove of other activities that endanger her health, particularly activities that would cause more serious harm than simply eating too many sweets. Similarly, Debbie's parents may admonish her under an extension of their rule prohibiting harm to their possessions. Debbie is unlikely to do any harm to the drain cleaner. On the other hand, the drain cleaner is one of her parents' possessions rather than one of Debbie's toys. Moreover, if Debbie spilled the drain cleaner, she would waste it, and she might harm other possessions of her parents that came in contact with the chemical. Therefore, Debbie's parents are likely to disapprove of Debbie's taking the drain cleaner out of concern for their possessions as well as concern for Debbie's safety.

Because the chemical could cause serious harm to Debbie and to her parents' possessions, I conclude that her parents will admonish her and will adopt a general rule prohibiting her from taking such bottles from cupboards.

B. An Example Raising Issues in Quasi-Contract

You probably have not studied the topic of quasi-contract, and will learn about it only as you read the following sample answer. For now, study the answer mainly for its form. Try to identify the passages in the sample answer that (1) state quick conclusions on matters that are not subject to debate and that simply set up other issues, (2) set forth issues or subissues, (3) summarize rules or subrules, (4) apply rules to facts, and (5) arrive at conclusions. Note the extent to which the sample answer presents arguments for both sides of the dispute and how the sample answer addresses remedies, as directed by the question, even though the answer finds no basis for liability after addressing that threshold issue.

Sample Exam Question

While jogging one morning, realtor Maria Reyes came upon the victim of an auto accident that had occurred a few minutes earlier. The victim was unconscious and was bleeding profusely from a severed artery. Reyes saved the victim's life by flagging down a motorist and by applying direct pressure to the severed artery during the ten-minute ride to the hospital. A paramedic would have charged $300 for providing a similar life-saving technique. Reyes's clothes were covered with blood, but they washed clean. Reyes herself was shaken and exhausted for a few hours after the incident. Reyes later demanded compensation from the victim. Discuss the potential liability and remedies.

Sample Answer

Liability in Quasi-Contract for Unjust Enrichment:
The unconscious victim could not expressly or through conduct communicate a promise to pay Reyes. Therefore, Reyes cannot recover on the basis of contract or promissory estoppel.

Reyes likely will bring an action in quasi-contract for restitution of the reasonable value of the benefit that she conferred on the victim. To recover on this theory, she must prove that she unjustly enriched the victim. Enrichment is a measurable benefit. Reyes clearly enriched the victim by rendering tangible first aid services and summoning help, thus saving the victim's life.

Reyes must also prove that it would be unjust for the victim to retain the benefits of the first-aid services without compensating Reyes for them. Reyes could prove this by showing that she had some relationship with the victim that led Reyes reasonably to expect compensation. However, the courts ordinarily presume that emergency services at the scene of an accident are provided gratuitously.

Reyes could overcome that presumption if she could show that she acted in a professional capacity when rendering the services or that the services she rendered were unusually burdensome or hazardous. Reyes cannot establish any expectation of compensation based on her profession: She is a realtor and is not in the business of charging for medical services.

Reyes might have a better chance of rebutting the presumption of gratuitous emergency services by showing that her services were so burdensome that she expected compensation. After all, she engaged in the physically demanding task of cradling an accident victim in a moving car for ten minutes while applying direct pressure to a bleeding artery. The physical and emotional distress of this event caused her to suffer exhaustion and distress for several hours. On the other hand, Reyes's actions posed little risk to her own safety, took relatively little time, and did not require special knowledge, skill, or training. Moreover, she likely would have felt distressed by the accident even if she had only witnessed the injury and had not acted to treat the victim.

Although this is a close question, the facts suggest that Reyes could not reasonably have expected compensation for her emergency services. Therefore, I conclude that Reyes cannot recover.

Remedies:
Assuming that Reyes could prove a claim for quasi-contract, she would be entitled to restitution measured by the reasonable value of the benefit

that she bestowed on the victim. The purpose of such relief would be to deny the unjust enrichment to the recipient of the benefit; therefore, whenever feasible, damages ought to be measured by the value that the recipient places on the benefit. If that is not feasible, a court may award damages based on the general market value of the benefit or on the out-of-pocket costs incurred by the provider of the benefit.

In this case, from the perspective of the victim, the value of the benefit bestowed by Reyes arguably is the value of the victim's life. A court would not use this value as the measure of the restitutionary relief, because it is relatively difficult to fix and because it is disproportionately greater than the effort expended by Reyes. Instead, the court probably would award the damages based on the general market value of Reyes's services. That measure is more nearly proportionate to Reyes's efforts, and it can easily be established by reference to the $300 fee that would have been charged by a paramedic. Alternatively, a court might award damages based on the actual costs incurred by Reyes, as measured by such things as inconvenience to Reyes and the cost of cleaning her jogging clothes.

Because the market-value remedy is more consistent with restitution, I conclude that a court would award $300 in damages if Reyes could establish a claim based on quasi-contract.

IV. EXERCISES

A. A Nonlegal Setting

To focus your attention mainly on the form of your answer, let's begin with a problem set in a familiar nonlegal setting. Imagine that you have formed the following outline from the cases set forth in Chapter 5, Section III.B.2:

> I. Parents limit high-school-age children's evening social activities to protect them from harm and to ensure that adequate time is reserved for rest and homework.
>
>   A. Child must inform parents of plans for social activities, including informing them by phone of new plans to move from one activity to another.
>
>   1. Example: In Case 1, Parents were unhappy when Child went to a pizza parlor after a football game without informing Parents of trip to a pizza parlor.
>
>   2. Example: In Case 2, Parents were content when Child went to a football game and then to a pizza parlor after informing Parents of those plans.
>
>   B. Child must return home from evening social activities by midnight, unless the event is an important family gathering.

1. Example: In Case 2, Parents were content when Child informed them of her plans and returned home shortly after 11 p.m.
2. Example: In Case 3, Child informed Parents of her activities but was admonished after coming home after midnight.
3. Exception: In Case 4, Child was permitted, and even required, to attend a wedding from which the family returned after midnight, where Parents participated and could monitor children's activities.

Now, identify and fully discuss the issues raised by the following facts, including all the elements of IRAC. Allow yourself 30 minutes to complete your answer and then compare your answer with the sample answer in Appendix B.

Essay Question

On Friday night, Lina, who is a junior in high school, went to the school dance with a date, Pat, after informing her parents of these plans. When Lina and Pat returned from the dance at 11:55 P.M., they parked in the driveway at Lina's house, within view of Lina's mother, Carmen, who was sitting in the living room and saw them arrive. While parked in the driveway, Lina and Pat talked, laughed, and held hands for 20 minutes. After Pat kissed Lina goodbye and drove away, Lina entered her house at 12:15 A.M.

On Saturday afternoon, Lina asked her parents whether Lina could go with friends to the high school basketball game, to watch Lina's brother play in the first of more than two dozen games in the basketball season. This first game is being played in another city, so Lina will ride in the car of another family, who plans to go out for a snack after the game and probably will not return Lina to her home until after midnight. Lina's father, Antonio, plans to attend some home games during the season, but neither parent plans to attend this first away game.

Fully discuss whether Lina's action on Friday and request on Saturday are consistent with her parents' rules regarding the social activities of a high-school-age child. For every issue that you identify, summarize the rule or subrule that helps to resolve that issue, apply the rule to the relevant facts, and reach a conclusion. Whenever possible, discuss both sides of the question.

B. Negligence: Application of Tort Law to Facts

Because you presumably have not studied tort law yet, I will provide you with some legal rules that could be derived from a number of cases that address the tort of negligence. I will then present an essay question that invites you to identify an issue or issues, to summarize the rule relating to each issue, to apply the rule to the facts—arguing both sides if possible—and to reach a reasonable conclusion. Allow yourself 60 minutes to complete your answer and then compare your answer with the sample answer in Appendix B.

LAW: YOU CAN ASSUME THAT THE FOLLOWING
RULES OF STATE LAW APPLY TO THIS PROBLEM:

An employer may be liable in tort for injuries caused by its employee's negligence for activities within the scope of the employee's work. The elements of a claim for negligence are a negligent act or omission that proximately causes injury. A negligent act or omission consists of a breach of a duty of care owed to another. A medical specialist owes a duty to patients to exercise at least the ordinary skill and care that is reasonable and customary within that medical specialty in this state. Proximate cause is a flexible doctrine that precludes liability if the relationship between negligence and an injury is so attenuated that it would be unfair to hold the negligent party responsible for the injury. Lack of proximate cause between a negligent act and an injury may stem from a break in that chain of causation through the intercession of a supervening cause, which is an unexpected intervening event that more directly produces the injury. Under the defense of assumption of the risk, a victim of negligence cannot recover if she had specific knowledge of a risk and voluntarily assumed the risk by her actions or choices. If liability and causation are otherwise shown, however, a tortfeasor must pay for all injuries sustained, even if the victim is unusually frail and susceptible to injury.

Essay Question

Kelly is an anesthesiologist employed by Samaritan, a private hospital. Kelly informed Rose, a patient scheduled for surgery to correct a bone deformity of her foot, of the advantages and risks associated with the three most appropriate general anesthetics. On the basis of relative costs, Rose rejected the safest but most expensive anesthetic, forane, in favor of a generally safe and more widely used anesthetic, ethane.

Samaritan protocols require anesthesiologists to administer general anesthesia only when assisted by qualified medical personnel. Kelly administered the general anesthesia to Rose without assistance, however, before the surgical team had arrived and while the circulating nurse was occupied with another patient. Unknown to anyone when she entered the hospital, Rose suffered from a rare, undiagnosed disorder of the nervous system that would produce a severe reaction to ethane, causing her heart to stop.

While administering general anesthesia, Kelly concentrated intensely on gauges on the equipment that measured Rose's intake of the anesthetic.

Kelly did not maintain visual contact with Rose or with equipment monitoring Rose's vital signs. As a consequence, Kelly failed to terminate the intake of anesthetic until ten seconds after the first visible signs of an adverse reaction from Rose. Although Rose was ultimately resuscitated, she suffered permanent brain damage because of an interruption of flow of oxygen to the brain during heart stoppage.

Discuss Samaritan's potential liability in tort, assuming no contractual waiver of rights. Discuss only issues raised by the facts of this question under the legal rules set forth before the question.

C. Offer: Application of Contract Law to Facts

Review your work in Exercise A in Chapter 6. You may have concluded that a general ad is not an offer under common law, partly because it lacks a quantity limitation and does not identify which customer is entitled to respond to the ad and bind the store by accepting. In the absence of such limitations, if such an ad were interpreted to be an offer that could be accepted by any of tens of thousands of customers who read it, the seller could be bound to sell many more units than it has in stock, resulting in liability for breach of numerous contracts. Because a reasonable person would not assume that a store was willing to subject itself to potentially unlimited liability, the ad is not reasonably interpreted to amount to an offer unless the ad is unusually definite and leaves nothing important left to negotiate. Terms that protect the seller from unlimited liability make it more likely that the ad is reasonably interpreted to be an offer. Indeed, perhaps general circumstances could convey the limitations and definiteness consistent with an offer.

The following midterm examination question focuses solely on whether a store has conveyed an offer to a consumer. The question is unusual in that it presents two different factual scenarios and asks you to compare them, applying the same rule to each. To the extent that you see facts in a single scenario that support arguments for both sides of the question of whether the ad is an offer, you should present those opposing arguments. The main point of the question, however, is to invite you to explain why one scenario is much more likely to be an offer than the other. Compare your answer with the sample answer in Appendix B.

 Essay Question: Products Offered for Sale Analyzed Under Common Law

Consider each of the numbered scenarios below and answer the question that follows:

(1) BetterBuy ("BB" for short) advertised a number of items for sale in the local newspaper. One part of the ad pictured a laptop computer

and stated "Great Price: HP Pavilion dv4t-5100 Entertainment Note-book PC laptop computer for $625 each during our Labor Day weekend sale, Saturday through Monday, limit one per customer." [You can refer to this product as "the ad PC," for short.]

(2) Jon walked into a BB store over Labor Day weekend and saw the PC on display, next to a sign identifying it as "HP Pavilion dv4t-5100 Entertainment Notebook PC laptop computer," for sale at "$625, Labor Day weekend special, Saturday through Monday, limit: one per customer," and with eight boxes underneath the shelf marked with the name of this computer. [You can refer to this product as "the store PC," for short.]

Discuss whether each of these is likely to be an offer, and explain why. Although this relates to a transaction in goods that would generally be governed by the UCC, you may assume that the UCC does not include a provision that would help determine whether either of these is an offer, leaving a gap that would be filled by the common law. Moreover, you can ignore any other statutes or administrative regulations that regulate ads or other practices of retail stores. Discuss only why each of the scenarios above is likely to be, or fail to be, an offer under common law.

Use this format: Summarize a helpful rule in one paragraph. Then, in a second paragraph, analyze the facts of scenario #1 in light of the rule, and reach a conclusion. Finally, in a third paragraph, analyze the facts of scenario #2 in light of the rule, and reach a conclusion. With respect to each scenario, you need not argue both sides if you believe the conclusion is clear. Your analyses should suggest that one scenario is more likely to be an offer than the other.

D. Contract Formation: Application of Contract Law to Facts

After you have studied contract formation, including consideration and the basics of offer and acceptance, work through the following sample exam question, which requires you to identify and discuss the issues. Compare your answer with the sample answer in Appendix B.

 Essay Question: Multiple Issues

Janice Penny ("JP" for short) is a wealthy owner of an art gallery. After purchasing a custom-built mansion for $2 million, she paid a landscaping design company $5,000 for detailed plans that called for lavish landscaping, a swimming pool, and an entertainment area in her huge backyard, in five phases of construction. After sending the plans and timing requirements to several landscaping contractors for bids, Penny received the lowest bid—$100,000—from Dreamscape Landscaping ("DL" for short).

JP responded to DL's bid with the following letter, dated October 8, which you may assume constitutes a counter-offer to DL's bid:

To Dreamscape Landscaping:

Based on the plans and deadlines for performance that I sent to you, and including the conditions set forth in this letter, I offer to hire you to perform the backyard landscaping at my new home at your bid price of $100,000. Under any contract we form, I will pay you $20,000 after your completion of each of the five phases of construction, but only if I approve the quality of your work on each completed phase. I will approve your work and pay for a phase of construction only if, in my sole judgment, your work meets my personal standards for the artistic quality and excellence appropriate for business and social events held at the home of an art gallery owner. You can accept by signing and returning this letter to the return address on my envelope.

Sincerely,
[signed by JP]

On October 10, DL received JP's letter and immediately sent a foreman to JP's mansion to collect soil samples to help plan for planting trees and shrubs and for excavating a pit for the pool. At this time, JP was at her art gallery. When JP's longtime housekeeper answered the door, the foreman announced the purpose of his visit. The housekeeper telephoned JP at the art gallery and informed her of the visit of DL's foreman and asked whether she should permit him to take soil samples.

Fully discuss whether JP and DL have formed an enforceable contract on the facts above, even before JP has responded to the housekeeper's question. If you identify more than one issue, discuss the issues in separate IRACs. For each IRAC, briefly and simply identify the issue; summarize the applicable rule in your own words under general common law principles; apply the rules to the facts, arguing both sides to the extent that you can; and state the conclusion that you believe is most likely. *Do not* discuss *offer* as an issue; you can assume that JP's letter of October 8 constitutes an offer on definite terms for some kind of transaction.

E. Unconscionability: Application of Contract Law to Facts

After you have studied unconscionability in your Contracts course, work through this sample exam question, which raises a single legal issue but offers plenty of ammunition for factually rich arguments and counterarguments. Compare your answer with the sample answer in Appendix B.

Essay Question: Single Issue—Unconscionability

Bill teaches engineering at a local university. He lives in a four-bedroom house in a nice neighborhood in the fictitious southwestern state of Calvada. The homeowner's association in Bill's neighborhood recently adopted a rule permitting any homeowner to paint their roof tiles or shingles with a special thick, white reflective paint to reduce air conditioning bills during the hot summer season. As a consequence, three roof treatment companies sent advertisements to residents of Bill's neighborhood. These companies advertised competitive contractual terms, warranting their high quality treatment for ten years, allowing payment in two to three monthly installments after the work is completed, and quoting a price range of $2,000-$3,000 for roofs in the neighborhood, depending on the precise size and shape of the roof of each house. The ads accurately stated that, in any house with average or higher use of air conditioning, the savings on energy bills will more than pay for the roofing treatment over the lifetime of the treatment.

A fourth company, Bill Busters ("BB") did not send advertisements but sent an employee, Jake, to each home on Saturday, making a "one-time special offer" to treat the roof tiles for $5,000. Jake visited Bill in this manner, urging Bill to sign a written contract with single-spaced type on one side of a single sheet of paper (with a carbon copy underneath). The form contract set forth all terms in the same typeface, as illustrated here: font and size. When Bill stated that he first wanted to compare the products and terms offered by other companies, Jake said: "Sir, if you hesitate, you will miss out on today's one-time offer. We are the best in the business. Tell you what, I'm crazy to do this, but I'm going to give you an extra $500 off and write in a price of $4,500 in the space here for the price." Jake filled in that price, signed at the bottom of the page, and then stated: "But I've got lots of houses to cover today, so you need to sign now or lose this great opportunity." Without reading the form contract, Bill then signed on the signature line at the bottom of the page. Jake took the top copy and provided Bill with the carbon copy.

The product described on the BB contract was effective but was on the lower end of quality for such roof treatments, although most people wouldn't understand the stated product specifications without first conducting some research. Depending on the roof and the air conditioning used, even this lower quality treatment might possibly generate $4,500 in energy savings over the lifetime of BB's treatment, which likely would require reapplication in seven to eight years. The contract did not include any express warranties on the treatment, and none would be implied under the common law of Calvada. The contract says nothing about dispute resolution. It requires advance payment by personal check when BB employees arrive to apply the treatment.

Bill later compared his contract with the advertised terms of other companies and now asks you whether he can "get out of" the BB contract. You may assume the following: (1) Jake's "sales puffing" did **not** constitute misrepresentation or duress, and (2) BB's treatment would consist primarily of services, so any dispute would be governed by the common law of Calvada, which adopts the majority approach of requiring both branches of unconscionability. Discuss only one issue in a single IRAC: whether the BB contract is unenforceable in its entirety for unconscionability. First, summarize the applicable rule. Then, in your fact analysis, discuss Bill's arguments for unconscionability, separating procedural and substantive arguments into different paragraphs, and then do the same for BB's counterarguments against unconscionablity. State whichever conclusion you believe is most strongly supported by the law and facts.

V. THE NEXT STEP

Other types of exam questions await you. Continue to the next chapter to explore further.

CHAPTER 11

Essay Questions of a Different Kind

Chapter 10 addressed in detail the kind of essay exam questions that are most typical in law school: fact-based questions with uncertain answers. Professors, however, are free to construct essay questions in any form they please, and the possibilities are endless.

One of my colleagues recently wrote a series of essay exam questions inspired by lines from one of his favorite American poets, and he preceded the questions with inspirational lines of poetry, which added some color to his supplementary facts. No book can prepare you for every curve that a professor might throw your way, but the unusual examples are rare. This chapter explores a few kinds of essay questions that differ from the traditional model explored in Chapter 10 but that nonetheless appear with some frequency.

I. FACT-BASED ESSAY QUESTION WITH A CERTAIN ANSWER

A. Explaining a Result Rather Than Arguing Both Sides

This book has advised you at several stages to gain comfort with uncertainty in the law and to argue both sides of a close question of law or the application of law to facts. Some essay questions, however, do contemplate a certain answer and invite the test-taker to use the IRAC formulation to identify issues and explain why the applicable legal rules apply to the facts to reach a certain conclusion or set of conclusions. A professor is most likely to compose this kind of question when an applicable set of rules work together in a complicated fashion, so that the professor wants to test your ability to navigate the rules without the distraction of arguing both sides of a close question.

After you graduate from law school, most states will require you to take and pass a bar exam as a prerequisite to obtaining a license to practice law.

In my experience, bar exam essay questions more frequently contemplate a "correct" answer or set of answers than do law school essay exams.

My memory of the essay questions from bar exams in two states is hazy after more than three decades, but I can remember one well enough to serve as a general example. This essay question set forth facts regarding offerings of evidence at trial and then asked about the admissibility of various items of evidence. For each item of evidence in issue, test-takers were expected to summarize the applicable rule or rules of evidence, apply it to facts that pointed fairly certainly in the direction of admissibility or nonadmissibility, and reach a certain correct result.

That each issue had a correct answer did not mean that the question was easy. To answer all of the issues within the allotted time required a solid grasp of the rules of evidence and well-honed skills of expression. Moreover, one of the issues required a knowledge and application of contract law to recognize that a party would be legally bound by a statement of apparent willingness to enter into a contract—regardless of whether that statement accurately and truthfully reflected the speaker's secret intentions—so that a different witness's testimony about that statement would not be classified as potentially inadmissible "hearsay." Although that question was tricky, it did contemplate a certain correct answer.

B. Recognizing and Reacting to Questions with Certain Answers

Some questions will provide you with a conclusion and ask you to explain how the conclusion follows from the law and the facts. Several years ago, for example, I gave an essay exam that began with this short warm-up question:

Question 1. Suggested Time Allocation: 5 minutes/Short Answer
Unknown to the owner of land, a tenant farmer ("TF") working on the land enters into an enforceable contract with an earth moving company, "EMC," to dig trenches on the land for an irrigation system for a fee of $2,000. When EMC presents TF with a bill for $2,000, TF refuses to pay, even though he is solvent. You may assume that EMC has enriched the owner by enhancing the value of the owner's land. Briefly explain why, given the facts of this case and the law in most states, EMC nonetheless does not have a strong claim against the **owner** for any recovery in quasi-contract. What legal element of the claim is missing and why? [Do not consider mechanics' liens, or any other law other than the quasi-contract claim. You need not discuss both sides of the question or address all the elements of IRAC; just answer the questions above in 1-3 sentences.]

This question required students to summarize the rules for recovery under that theory and to explain why one of the elements of the rule could not be satisfied by the facts. Based on the cases we had studied, I hoped that students would note that (1) a claim in quasi-contract requires proof of unjust enrichment, and (2) although EMC clearly enriched the owner, the owner is not retaining that enrichment unjustly because EMC expected payment not from the owner but from TF, who is solvent and remains obligated by contract. In this question, I not only contemplated a certain conclusion, I identified the conclusion that I wanted students to support.

Other essay questions of this sort might not identify a conclusion for you or even inform you that the question most likely has a single certain answer. Instead, it will look like a traditional essay question of the type discussed in Chapter 10: It will state the facts of some event or transaction, and will end with a general prompt asking you to analyze the rights and liabilities of the parties. However, if the facts do not raise close questions that support reasonable arguments for both sides, then they do not raise "issues" in the sense discussed in Chapter 10, and your task is one of identifying the applicable rules and applying the rules to the facts to reach a certain conclusion. In some cases, your professor might have chosen this format as the best way to test your knowledge of a complicated area of the law.

C. Example: The Battle of the Forms

For half a century, law students have struggled to master the complicated provisions of § 2-207 of the Uniform Commercial Code (UCC). Although the private organization that recommends the code to state legislatures has proposed a simplified revision, state legislatures have not been enthusiastic about the package of proposed revisions, so the commonly enacted text remains as follows (except for omission of a phrase not relevant to the example that follows):

§ 2-207. Additional Terms in Acceptance or Confirmation.

(1) A definite and seasonable expression of acceptance . . . which is sent within a reasonable time operates as an acceptance even though it states terms additional to or different from those offered or agreed upon, unless acceptance is expressly made conditional on assent to the additional or different terms.

(2) The additional terms are to be construed as proposals for addition to the contract. Between merchants such terms become part of the contract unless:

(a) the offer expressly limits acceptance to the terms of the offer;

(b) they materially alter it; or

(c) notification of objection to them has already been given or is given within a reasonable time after notice of them is received.

(3) Conduct by both parties which recognizes the existence of a contract is sufficient to establish a contract for sale although the writings of the parties do not otherwise establish a contract. In such case the terms of the particular contract consist of those terms on which the writings of the parties agree, together with any supplementary terms incorporated under any other provisions of this Act.

If I decided to test students on these provisions, I would be inclined to set forth facts that supported arguments for both sides on one or more issues, such as facts that created a dispute about whether additional terms in an acceptance would materially alter the offer under subsection 2(b) of the statute.

Even without facts that created a reasonable dispute on such a matter, however, an exam question could well test a student's working knowledge of the statute if it did no more than require the student to trace the manner in which various statutory requirements applied to facts to reach a set of certain conclusions. Consider, for example, the following sample essay question and answer, in a course in which the professor allows students access to the text of the UCC during the exam and expects citation to its sections:

Sample Essay Question

On January 7, Seller received from Buyer a mailed offer, on a printed form, to buy factory machine parts. On the first line of the form, directly after the printed term "Purchase order form," Buyer had written the following message by hand: "10 #BK-1000 machine parts, at your current catalog price, for delivery at our Newtown factory within 30 days." The purchase order form said nothing about dispute resolution or warranties.

On January 7, Seller sent a printed acknowledgment form, with a copy of the purchase order attached, with the handwritten message: "Your attached order is accepted, conditioned on your agreement to the printed terms on this form." Among the printed terms on the form were provisions (1) requiring private arbitration of any dispute arising out of the transaction, and (2) disclaiming all express and implied warranties. Buyer did not respond, Seller shipped the machine parts within two weeks, and Buyer accepted delivery of the parts a few days later, paying for them on delivery.

When Buyer installed a few of the parts later that week, however, the parts did not perform properly, slowing down the production line. Buyer threatened to bring suit in state court unless Seller replaced the goods with nondefective ones. Seller denied any liability and asserted that Buyer had waived its right to bring suit in court. Fully discuss the law and facts that apply to this dispute.

Sample Essay Answer
Acceptance of Buyer's Written Offer

The machine parts are movable personal property; therefore, this is a "transaction in goods" governed by Article 2 of the UCC rather than common law principles (UCC § § 2-102, 2-105). In contrast to the common law mirror-image rule, UCC § 2-207(1) recognizes a response to an offer as an acceptance, even if it contains additional or different terms, if it is a definite and "seasonable" expression of acceptance and if it does not expressly condition acceptance on the offeror's agreement to the additional or different terms. Such an express condition would make the response a rejection and counteroffer rather than an acceptance. A response is seasonable if sent within a time agreed or within a reasonable time (UCC § 1-204).

The question assumes that Buyer's purchase order is an offer. In the absence of Buyer's stating a time for acceptance, Seller's response time was clearly "seasonable," because Seller mailed it the same day as received, well within a reasonable time in a transaction calling for delivery within a month. Moreover, Seller appeared to definitely express acceptance with the phrase: "Your attached order is accepted." However, Seller then triggered the final proviso to UCC § 2-207(1) by expressing that Seller's acceptance was conditioned on Buyer's agreement to Seller's printed terms. Those printed terms include terms that were not in Buyer's offer, including terms relating to warranties and dispute resolution.

Consequently, because Seller insisted on Buyer's agreement to those additional terms, Seller's response is a rejection and counteroffer rather than an acceptance, even under the liberal provisions of § 2-207(1).

Contract Through Conduct

UCC § 2-207(3) governs conduct by the parties that arguably manifests their agreement if their forms fail to result in agreement under subsection 1. Subsection 3 states that if the writings do not establish a contract, the parties' conduct may nonetheless reflect a mutual intent to enter into a contract. The terms of such a contract by conduct will be those on which the writings agree, supplemented by "gap-filler" provisions of the UCC.

In this case, Seller's conduct of delivering the machine parts and Buyer's conduct of accepting delivery and paying for the goods constitute nearly every facet of performance and thus clearly reflect an intent to contract and the recognition of a contractual relationship. The contract of the parties will include the subject matter, quantity, price, and place of delivery on which the two forms of the parties agreed. The forms, however, did not agree on seller's requirement of private arbitration or disclaimer of warranties. Neither of these terms would become part of the agreement under § 2-207(3), because no gap-filler term of the UCC would require arbitration, and because UCC § 2-314 implies a warranty of merchantability in a sale of goods by a merchant of goods of that kind, unless the parties validly agree to disclaim it. Seller obviously is a merchant of these machine parts because it has a catalog listing these parts and their price, and thus "deals" in those goods under UCC § 2-104.

Consequently, the parties have a contract on the terms of Buyer's offer, and Buyer can assert his claim of breach of implied warranty in state court.

You can see that this essay answer is fairly sophisticated, even though it does not present any close questions on the facts that lead to any uncertainty in conclusions, and even though the question avoids application of subsection 2 entirely and avoids some of the thornier ambiguities in the statute.

Notice the organization of the statement of the rules and the fact application. This exam answer largely reflects a choice of aggregating and consolidating its statement of related rules before applying them to the facts. In the discussion of the first issue, for example, the first paragraph summarizes all the rules contained within subsection 1 of the statute, before applying them to the relevant facts in the second paragraph. The second issue is slightly more complex in organization, but it generally adopts the same approach of consolidating the rules in subsection 3 before applying them to the facts. The fact analysis of this issue requires some brief references to secondary rules in the UCC; nonetheless, even those references are part of an application of a basic rule about gap-filling stated in the first paragraph.

Thus, each of the issues contains a single IRAC: After identifying the issue in a section heading, the rules, application to facts, and conclusion are each set forth in a paragraph, with only minor deviations.

A different writer might have reasonably chosen a method of organization that separated the legal rules and fact applications into more numerous IRACs. For example, under the second section heading relating to a contract by conduct, the answer might have stated subsection 2's recognition of contractual intent through conduct and applied that to the facts, before then stating subsection 3's rule regarding the content of such an implied contract and then applying that rule to relevant facts.

D. Exercise: UCC § 2-207

Carefully study the provisions of UCC § 2-207 (reproduced in the previous section), which you can consult during the exam. Relying solely on those provisions, answer the following question in IRAC format in 45 minutes, looking for statutory terms and facts that lead to certain conclusions rather than arguments on both sides of a close question. Cite subsections of § 2-207 that supply relevant rules, and fully explain your reasoning. Compare your answer with that in Appendix C.

 Essay Question

On January 7, Seller received from Buyer a mailed offer on a printed form to buy factory machine parts. On the first line of the form, directly after the printed term "Purchase order form," Buyer had written the following message by hand: "10 #BK-1000 machine parts, guaranteed to process 1,000 units per hour, at your current catalog price, for delivery at our Newtown factory within 30 days." The purchase order form said nothing about dispute resolution.

On January 7, Seller sent a printed acknowledgment form, with a copy of the purchase order attached, with the handwritten message: "Your attached order is accepted. Expect delivery within two weeks." Among the printed terms on the form was a provision requiring private arbitration of any dispute arising out of the transaction. On the same day that Buyer received the acknowledgment form, Buyer read the form and sent an e-mail to Seller stating: "We object to mandatory private arbitration and reserve the right to bring any legal claims in state court."

Seller shipped the machine parts within two weeks, and Buyer accepted delivery of the parts a few days later, paying for them on delivery. When Buyer installed a few of the parts later that week, however, the parts did not perform properly, resulting in the processing of only 500 units per hour. Buyer threatened to bring suit in state court unless Seller replaced the goods with nondefective ones. Seller asserted that Buyer had waived its right to bring suit in court and that any dispute must be resolved through private arbitration.

Fully discuss whether the parties formed a contract and whether it requires disputes to be resolved in private arbitration. You may assume that both parties are merchants and that this is a transaction in goods to which the UCC applies, and thus you need not discuss those matters. Focus your answer on analyses that provide you with clear conclusions to the issues, but fully explain how you arrive at your conclusions through the law and the facts.

II. ESSAY QUESTIONS WITHOUT SUBSTANTIAL FACT ANALYSIS

Some essay questions will not be set in the context of a dispute and thus will not present facts for analysis in IRAC format. In most cases, questions such as these will invite you to discuss the law in the abstract. Following are brief discussions of some of the most common types of questions in this category.

A. Explanation of the Legal Doctrine

In some cases, the examiner will ask you to summarize the law on a fairly narrow topic, sometimes by comparing a rule to a posited change in the law, such as in the following examples:

- Explain the requirement of reciprocal inducement as an element of the doctrine of consideration.
- The courts of State X have just changed the common law by abandoning the long-standing defense of contributory negligence and replacing it with a system of pure comparative negligence. Explain to someone who is unfamiliar with these terms how the law has changed in State X.
- How would the following fictitious statute change the law of our state on . . . ?

In answering such a question, you would essentially summarize the law in the same way that you would address the "rule" element of IRAC in a fact-based essay question. Because the question does not ask you to apply the law to the facts of a dispute, less time is likely to be allocated to such a question than to one that requires application of the law to facts. Alternatively, if you are allotted generous time for such a question, your professor likely expects you to discuss the rule in greater detail than ordinarily would be possible if the problem also required fact analysis.

Questions in this category do not appear on exams as frequently as fact-based questions, because they mainly test your comprehension and memory of legal doctrine without also measuring the analytic skills associated with identifying issues and applying rules to new facts that you have not previously studied and analyzed. Nonetheless, if you have time, you can maximize the credit you receive by illuminating your explanation of legal doctrine with your own fact-based illustration. For example, after explaining that contributory negligence would bar a plaintiff from all recovery if the plaintiff contributed to her own injuries to any degree, and that comparative negligence would simply reduce the plaintiff's recovery by a percentage associated with the plaintiff's proportionate fault, you could illustrate how each doctrine would operate in a case in which 25 percent of the fault for the plaintiff's injuries was attributable to the plaintiff's own negligence.

B. Exercise: International Sale of Goods

In an international sales course, you likely will compare provisions of two sales codes: the Uniform Commercial Code (UCC) and the U.N.

Convention on Contracts for the International Sales of Goods (CISG). Study the following provisions of the UCC and CISG, and then give yourself ten minutes to answer the question that follows. You may consult the code provisions when you answer the question. Compare your answer with the sample answer in Appendix C.

Code Provisions:

Uniform Commercial Code (applies if the parties opt out of the CISG and choose the UCC)

UCC § 2-601. Buyer's Rights on Improper Delivery
[Subject to some exceptions], if the goods . . . fail *in any respect* to conform to the contract, the buyer may (a) reject the whole . . . . [italics added]

UCC § 2-711. Buyer's Remedies in General . . .
(1) Where . . . the buyer rightfully rejects . . . then with respect to any goods involved, the buyer may cancel [the contract and may recover damages as defined by the Act].

U.N. Convention on Contracts for the International Sale of Goods (applies to many international sales contracts, unless the parties opt out of it)

CISG art. 25
A breach of contract committed by one of the parties is fundamental if it results in such detriment to the other party as substantially to deprive him of what he is entitled to expect under the contract . . . .

CISG art. 46
. . .
(2) If the goods do not conform with the contract, the buyer may require delivery of substitute goods only if the lack of conformity constitutes a fundamental breach . . . .

CISG art. 49
(1) The buyer may declare the contract avoided:
(a) if the failure by the seller to perform any of his obligations under the contract or this Convention amounts to a fundamental breach of contract; or . . . .

 Essay Question: Negotiating Contractual Choice of Law

Your client, a seller of goods from California, is negotiating a sales contract with a buyer, a chain of retail stores in China. Your client, the seller, is nervous about the possibility that the buyer may reject delivered goods that fail to conform to contract description in even minor ways, after the goods have been transported thousands of miles. You could try to negotiate a contract provision that restricts the buyer's right to reject, while still allowing the buyer to claim money damages for minor nonconformities, but you don't want to draw attention to this topic during negotiations. Consequently, you want to identify which sales code would most benefit your client if its default rules are left to address the issue of the buyer's right to reject nonconforming goods.

If this international sales contract does not opt out of the CISG, the CISG will automatically apply. Do you prefer the contract to be governed by the CISG, or should you try to negotiate a clause that opts out of the CISG and chooses the UCC (as enacted in Californa) as the governing law? Explain.

C. Critique and Policy Analysis

A more sophisticated answer might be required if an essay question asks you to critically examine a rule, sometimes by asking whether you would favor judicial or legislative action to change it. For example, consider the following question about punitive damages, which are damages above and beyond compensation for actual losses, designed to punish a party for egregious conduct and to deter others from engaging in such conduct:

> Critically evaluate the general American rule excluding punitive damages in claims based solely on breach of contract. Do you favor retaining or changing the rule? Explain your position.

Even in a more traditional fact-based essay question, you will often illuminate your statement of a legal rule with an explanation of the policies that support it; however, you normally will not take the time to critique the merits of the rule. A question such as the one posed here, however, invites you to weigh the policy justifications for a rule against its weaknesses and against the merits of an alternative rule. Unless past exam questions and model answers suggest a different format, the following format is a good starting place: (1) Explain the merits of the rule, considering policy justifications that you have discussed in class; (2) critique the rule by explaining how the rule fails to advance important policies or otherwise leads to negative consequences; and (3) use a proposed alternative rule as a foil to argue that the rule should either be retained or rejected.

In response to this sample question, for example, a sophisticated answer might explain that the current rule excluding punitive damages for breach of contract reduces the level of risk and uncertainty in contracting so that honest parties are not dissuaded from entering into contracts. Moreover, limiting damages to compensation will often allow a party to an ongoing contract to engage in the economically efficient breach of reallocating its resources to a more profitable and productive use, after having compensated the victim of breach for actual losses caused by the breach. On the other hand, the student might also point out that a blanket prohibition of punitive damages fails to recognize the moral value of keeping promises, and fails to deter a party from breaching a contract for the sole purpose of maliciously injuring the other party rather than reallocating resources to a more productive use. For this reason, the student might argue in favor of a limited exception to the general rule, permitting punitive damages for breaches of contract in limited circumstances.

If your research suggests that some of your professors might include such a question on an exam, you will be grateful for having paid close attention in class when the professor led discussion about the policy considerations underlying legal rules, or when he or she fostered critical commentary on the law. When reviewing such courses, take some extra time with your study group to explore the policy justifications for rules discussed in your course, and to identify legal rules that your professor might view as suitable subjects for critique.

III. TAKE-HOME AND PERFORMANCE EXAMS

Some professors will permit students to complete an examination within an extended period of time, such as within 8, 24, or 48 hours, outside of the classroom, and with full access to course materials. Their reasons for doing so, and the type of answer they expect, probably fall largely into two categories: (1) relieving students from intense time pressure, or (2) providing students with the opportunity, albeit with considerable time pressure, to produce a document that is more formal than an in-class essay.

A. Easing the Time Pressure

Some professors believe that in-class law exams of three or four hours impose an unfair disadvantage on students who are bright and well prepared but who need more time to think the problems through, plan their answers, and express themselves clearly. Certainly, the professor could ease the time pressure by cutting the exam in half while still allowing three or four hours; however, reducing the scope of the exam is difficult if the professor wishes to test most or all of the major issues covered in the course.

Consequently, some professors will compose a take-home exam that is similar to an in-class exam but will then permit students to take it home for an extended period of time, such as 24 hours. One of my colleagues hands out such exams in the late afternoon, and he advises students to read the problem, plan the analysis, prepare an outline, and then "sleep on it" before writing out their answers the next day. His questions will be only slightly more complicated than those in an in-class exam, such as through the addition of a judicial opinion in the exam materials, with which the students must work.

My colleague hopes that the students will not "pull an all-nighter" but will have the luxury of sufficient time to think about the exam at some length before writing, and then will have sufficient time to write an essay answer that is normal in scope and format but is more clearly legible, well organized, and well composed than might be possible under the intense time pressure of an in-class exam. However, he notes that most students, feeling the pressure of competition from other students, fill nearly every hour of the 24-hour period, creating a more lengthy and formal document than he required. Another colleague allows students eight hours to take exams that are similar to an in-class exam. He reports that students, relieved of intense time pressure, produce answers that are similar in scope to an in-class exam answer, but with noticeably better writing and organization.

If you have a take-home exam that allows 24 hours or more, you should not allow the exam-writing task to expand to fill the entire time allotted to you, lest you exhaust yourself just before you face other exams. If the exam really is designed to be answered well within the allotted time period without skipping meals, losing sleep, or falling behind in your preparation for other exams, schedule your time so that you finish the exam with time to spare, without making sacrifices that might jeopardize your health or your preparedness for other exams.

Specifically, if your professor has designed the take-home exam to relieve you of time pressure, devise a schedule that allows for efficient but not panicky work. As intended by your professor, allow yourself a generous amount of time to read, analyze, and think through the problem. At the same time, however, start working early, eliminate distractions, maintain a sharp focus, and set some relatively ambitious goals for completing your answer with several hours to spare.

With the hours you have retained in reserve, you can review your answer for substance and revise it for style (or deal with some malfunction of your computer or printer). Your professor administered this type of exam precisely because he or she wants a product that can be more easily read than the typical in-class essay answer. Consequently, you likely will earn a better grade by leaving yourself time for review and revision, rather than by researching the problem to death and writing a lengthy, disorganized answer at the last minute on two hours of sleep.

B. Performance Exams with Sophisticated Answers

I use the term *performance exams* to refer to exams that seek to mirror the types of assignments that a recent graduate might encounter in practice, such as an assignment to research a problem and produce a formal office memorandum that analyzes the problem. Rather than set forth a summary of the facts of a problem, such an exam might provide you with a file that contains documents—such as notes from client and witness interviews, excerpts from deposition testimony, provisions from a contract, or a police report—from which you are required to synthesize facts or at least factual assertions of various parties or witnesses.

Although the examiner would not likely turn you and your classmates loose in the library to research the applicable law, he or she might create a limited library for each student by providing a statute and group of cases that must be read and synthesized. Finally, the exam question might require you to draft a formal document, such as an office memorandum or perhaps a reply to a motion for summary judgment that has been presented in the exam materials.

Although exams of this nature are still rare in first-year courses, they should be familiar to any first-year law student, because they would be quite similar to assignments given to students in a typical first-year Legal Writing course. The main difference is time pressure. A Legal Writing student normally would get a few weeks to work on an office memo assignment and probably would be required to produce a second draft after receiving constructive criticism on the first draft. In the context of a take-home exam, however, the student will have one shot at producing a final draft under much greater time pressure, perhaps 8 to 48 hours.

There is no magic trick to performing well on such an exam. If you have followed the advice of previous chapters, by briefing and synthesizing cases and by preparing your own course outlines, and if you have worked conscientiously in your Legal Writing class, you will have developed all the skills necessary to perform well on this kind of take-home exam.

IV. THE NEXT STEP

You now have an introduction to most of the kinds of essay questions you might come across in law school. An increasing number of professors, however, are supplementing essay questions with objective questions, such as true–false or multiple-choice questions, and some of them give exams that consist entirely of such objective questions. For your final lesson on law school exams, the next chapter details how to maximize your scores on objective questions.

CHAPTER 12

Objective Questions

I. TRUE–FALSE AND MULTIPLE-CHOICE QUESTIONS

True–false and multiple-choice questions are often known as *objective questions*, probably because they are meant to have a single correct answer and thus do not require individualized subjective evaluation by the examiner. Some questions that solicit a short textual response might also be objective in this sense; however, questions that require you to "fill in the blank" with a single, uniquely correct word or phrase are rare in law school. Therefore, this chapter addresses only true–false and multiple-choice questions.

These types of objective questions typically require you to know the law in greater detail than might be necessary to respond to an essay question. In an essay answer, you can display your analytic skills by summarizing the law at a fairly general level and by explaining how that law applies to specific facts and how the facts can support arguments for both sides. An objective question, however, must have a single unambiguously correct answer, which means that it cannot turn on a close question of fact. It could be based on an application of a simple legal rule to facts that clearly satisfy or violate the rule, but most questions of that type would be too easy to serve as a good testing vehicle. To make an objective question appropriately intellectually demanding, the unambiguously correct answer often follows from a statement of law that requires you to understand some of the finer or more complicated points of law that you studied.

Additionally, objective questions typically call for particularly focused and critical reading. To be brutally honest, whereas the typical essay question will helpfully provide you with ammunition to develop a full response, some true–false and multiple-choice questions are designed to lead you astray and then trip you up. They do this by making statements that are temptingly attractive in most respects and thus look like good candidates for a "true" answer or for the one correct response to a multiple-choice question; they nonetheless contain a falsehood or element of poor reasoning that you are expected to detect with a highly specific knowledge of the law and a careful reading of the assertion.

Therefore, you should read objective questions carefully, critically, and even suspiciously, ready to find a flaw. Obviously, you should not go overboard and imagine a flaw in a perfectly sound assertion, but that risk is minor compared to the greater tendency to miss a flaw planted by your professor that is designed to make the statement false.

Even if you are primarily interested in learning more about multiple-choice questions, do not skip over the next section addressing true–false questions. For the most part, a multiple-choice question requires you to engage in the same reading and thinking process for each of four or five alternatives as does a true–false question. Consequently, nearly every point discussed next about true–false questions will also apply to multiple-choice questions.

II. TRUE–FALSE QUESTIONS

A. Look for the Flaw in a Statement with Mostly True Assertions

In a true–false question, the statement about the law typically will be multifaceted. You are expected to mark it as false if it is inaccurate in any respect. In other words, it is "true" only if it is accurate in every respect.

To take a nonlegal example, a true–false question might include the following assertions about dogs:

> With few exceptions, dogs have four legs, a tail, teeth suitable for a carnivore's diet, and broad, webbed feet like a duck's, for efficient paddling in water.

Although this statement contains mostly accurate information, and although many dogs are pretty good swimmers, their paws are not accurately described as "broad, webbed feet like a duck's." Thus, you would mark this statement "false," even though the several accurate assertions might have generated some expectation in you that the statement would be true. A moment's reflection suggests that your professor can draft a true–false question in a legal context that is clearly accurate in several respects but contains a single flaw that requires a sophisticated grasp of the law to identify.

B. But Recognize That the Statement Might Be True in All Respects

Although you should look carefully for one or more flaws in every statement, if you find none after a critical reading, your best judgment must be that it is a true statement. In fact, just as your professor might dress up a false statement to look attractively valid, he or she might test your ability to recognize the accuracy of a perfectly true statement that contains some surprising information. Consider, for example, the following statement:

> In our state, punitive damages are not authorized for a claim based solely on breach of contract, even if the defendant breached the contract with the malicious intent to harm the other party.

The second clause, beginning with "even if," is designed to sound extreme, to tempt a student to conclude that the statement is false. Nonetheless, the entire statement is true in many states, so long as the defendant was liable only in contract and not also in tort, as the statement posits.

To similar effect is the following statement:

> By enacting valid legislation that sets forth a different statutory rule, a state legislature can replace even a long-standing common law rule expressed in precedent of the state's highest court.

Again, this statement sounds extreme in its referring to the replacement "even" of long-standing precedent of the highest court of the state. Nonetheless, it is unflawed because the state legislature has the authority to replace a common law rule with a contrary statutory rule. A state constitution might occasionally set forth an exception to this general rule, but the modifier "valid" in the statement rules out the possibility of unconstitutional legislation.

C. True–False Questions with Fact Patterns

Some true–false assertions will be preceded by a fact pattern, similar to a short essay question. The true–false assertion following the fact pattern can then do more than advance an abstract statement of law; it can also incorporate an implicit application of law to facts by asserting a conclusion. You are expected to identify the applicable law and apply it to the facts to reach a conclusion and thus to evaluate whether the asserted conclusion is true or false.

Here is a simple example, loosely inspired by real cases that appear in many first-year casebooks in a Contracts course:

> 17. *W* entered into a contract with *B* in which *B* agreed for a fee to supply water from *B*'s well to *W*'s established and profitable but remote factory. *B* knew that *W*'s factory would cease operating if the water supply were interrupted. After performing the contract without incident for one month,

a feud developed between *W* and *B*, and *B* intentionally cut off the flow of water to *W*'s factory for the purpose of causing *W* to suffer economic losses. In a lawsuit, *W* proved with certainty that *B* intentionally breached the contract without excuse, causing *W* to suffer losses, including lost profits, but *W* did not prove facts supporting any tort or other type of claim. Thus, remedies must be based solely on the claim for breach of contract, and the contract does not address remedies for breach. Is the following statement true or false?

In most states, the court will authorize the jury to exercise discretion to award punitive damages to *W*, in addition to calculating and awarding damages designed to compensate for actual losses.

This question requires you to know the rule in most states that punitive damages are not authorized for even an intentional breach of contract, regardless of whether the breaching party acted for the purpose of reallocating resources to a more productive use or simply to hurt the other party. The result would be different if *W* had pleaded and proved a tort claim, such as intentional infliction of emotional distress, but the facts preclude that possibility. Thus, an application of the majority rule to the facts reveals the assertion in the question to be false.

The assertion probably would entice some students to mark it as true, because it advances what sounds like a reasonable course of action on the facts: simply granting discretion to the jury to determine whether punitive damages are appropriate. Nonetheless, you would be expected to know that the law of most states draws a bright line between torts and contracts, wholly excluding punitive damages on claims that the law has categorized as solely ones for breach of contract.

Fact patterns are more commonly found in multiple-choice questions than in true–false questions, because they represent a great investment of time and space to test the truth or falsity of a single assertion. As a compromise, some professors will present a sort of hybrid true–false/multiple-choice question, one that associates several assertions with a single fact pattern, but that—unlike a multiple-choice question—could have more than one true assertion, or none at all. For example, the fact pattern in the preceding illustration could be followed by several assertions:

17-22. *W* entered into a contract with *B* in which *B* agreed for a fee to supply water. . . . Under the law in force in most states, is each of the following statements true or false?

17. *W* cannot recover damages for lost profits, because compensatory damages are awarded for unavoidable, foreseeable losses that *W* proves with reasonable certainty, but not including lost profits, even if they are proved under those standards.

18. The court would not authorize the jury to award damages for emotional distress, because no state's law permits such damages for breach of contract in any circumstances.

19. The court would not authorize the jury to award punitive damages to *W*, because the contract did not include a clause in which the parties agreed that the victim of breach would be entitled to punitive damages in addition to compensation for actual losses.

20. *W* would be entitled to damages for the emotional distress that he suffered as a result of the breach, because such damages can be recovered in most states for breach of a contract designed to protect emotional sensibilities.

21. The jury would not be authorized to award punitive damages to *W*, because damages for future lost profits suffered by a new enterprise are exceedingly difficult to prove with reasonable certainty, if the court would allow such proof at all.

All of these assertions are false. I drafted them that way to help illustrate the various kinds of flaws that you might find in an assertion. An explanation of the flaw embedded in each response follows. The relevant response is repeated before the explanation for your convenience.

1. Most Elements of the Statement of Law Are Correct, but the Conclusion and at Least One Element of the Law Are Incorrect

17. *W* cannot recover damages for lost profits, because compensatory damages are awarded for unavoidable, foreseeable losses that *W* proves with reasonable certainty, but not including lost profits, even if they are proved under those standards.

Imagine this description of a chocolate dessert: "You will love this rich chocolate cake, topped with creamy dark chocolate frosting, on which are sprinkled chopped walnuts, and over which is poured a generous helping of spicy tomato sauce." Now you wouldn't be fooled, would you? True, most people would find the chocolate cake, the frosting, and the chopped nuts to be appealing, but few people would accept the conclusion that "you will love" a chocolate cake covered with spicy tomato sauce. Three out of four elements hit the mark, but a single false note is sufficient to ruin the dish.

Similarly, assertion 17 might sound attractive to some students, because its statement of law correctly summarizes three limitations on contracts remedies: Money damages generally are awarded only for those injuries that were reasonably foreseeable at the time of contracting, unavoidable at the time of breach, and later proved with reasonable certainty. The final clause, however, erroneously excludes damages for lost profits, which can be recoverable—at least on behalf of an established enterprise like *W*'s factory—if the other criteria are met. The statement about the law is only as strong as its weakest link; one flaw among a series of correct elements makes the entire statement of law false.

2. The Legal Rule Is Incorrect, Even Though the Conclusion May Be Correct

18. The court would not authorize the jury to award damages for emotional distress, because no state's law permits such damages for breach of contract in any circumstances.

It is easy to see what is wrong with the following statement: "The sun will surely rise tomorrow morning, because it revolves around the earth every day." Although you can readily accept the conclusion that the sun will rise tomorrow, you know that it will do so because the earth rotates on its axis daily and not because the sun revolves around the earth. The accurate conclusion does not establish the accuracy of a proposition; the supporting premise must be accurate as well.

Similarly, assertion 18 almost certainly states a correct conclusion, because the facts of the question do not describe proof of any emotional distress, and because such damages would not be recoverable for breach of this type of commercial contract under the correct legal rule, which is stated accurately for most professors' tastes in assertion 20. The statement of the law in assertion 18 is incorrect, however, because many states will permit damages for emotional distress in contract actions in unusual circumstances. Unlike most states' bright-line rule against awarding punitive damages in contract actions, the rule against granting damages for emotional distress is commonly subject to an exception for breach of contracts designed to protect emotional sensibilities. A correct conclusion is not sufficient to make the entire assertion true; a flawed statement of the legal rule that produces the conclusion will render the entire assertion false.

3. A Correct Conclusion Is Purportedly Explained by Facts That Would Be Relevant Only Under an Inaccurate Implicit Legal Premise

19. In most states, the court would not authorize the jury to award punitive damages to *W*, because the contract did not include a clause in which the parties agreed that the victim of breach would be entitled to punitive damages in addition to compensation for actual losses.

Imagine that you and I met on a college football field and that you held a football upright on the ground at one end of the field, inviting me to kick it through the uprights at the opposite end of the field, 100 yards away. We both know that I cannot possibly kick a football that far, so you would reject my implicit boast if I responded, "I'm sorry, I can't kick it that far today because I'm wearing my dress shoes rather than my tennis shoes." You were calling my bluff from the outset, so you would have no trouble accepting the conclusion that "I can't kick it that far," but you would reject my factual explanation, which seeks to advance the implicit proposition that I could kick the football to the other end of the field if only I were wearing my tennis shoes. In truth, the style of shoes that I am wearing is irrelevant, because I would be unable to kick a football the length of the field with any type of footwear.

Similarly, assertion 19 states the correct conclusion, but it seeks to explain that conclusion with facts that are irrelevant. Assertion 19 is tempting because it implicitly advances the following proposition of law, which sounds like it might be correct: "Even if punitive damages could not be awarded in the absence of a penalty clause in the contract, the court will enforce an agreement by the parties to award punitive damages for breach of contract." A well-prepared student, however, would know that a damages clause in a contract would be unenforceable if punitive in nature. Consequently, the absence of a penalty clause in the contract is irrelevant to the analysis and should not be viewed as a determinative factor; under the correct standard, punitive damages would not be awarded for breach of contract, regardless of whether the contract included a penalty clause.

4. The Statement of the Law Is Correct in the Abstract, but It Produces a Different Conclusion When Applied to the Facts

20. W would be entitled to damages for the emotional distress that he suffered as a result of the breach, because such damages can be recovered in most states for breach of a contract designed to protect emotional sensibilities.

The following assertion sounds innocent enough: "You don't need a heavy coat for our walk today, because sweatpants and a sweatshirt will keep you warm on a mild, sunny day." The general proposition in the second clause of this assertion sounds accurate. Suppose that the facts show, however, that the weather outside is bone-numbingly cold, with temperatures below freezing and with an additional wind-chill factor. The conclusion in the opening clause of the assertion ("You don't need a heavy coat . . .") is inaccurate in light of these facts, regardless of whether the proposition that follows it—which assumes different facts—is accurate when viewed in isolation.

Similarly, the second clause in assertion 20 accurately states the legal rule in most states regarding recovery of damages for emotional distress, because it assumes a contract that is designed to protect emotional sensibilities, where damages for emotional distress would be foreseeable. Students of contract law would know that this principle is limited to exceptional circumstances, such as emotional distress stemming from an egregious breach of a contract to provide dignified funeral services for a departed spouse of the contracting party. That narrow rule would not be satisfied by the question's facts, however, which describe a standard commercial contract; therefore, the conclusion stated in the opening clause of the assertion is inaccurate. Assertion 20 is false because of its flawed application of the law to the facts of the question.

5. Accurate Statement of the Law Is Irrelevant to a Correct Conclusion and Thus Does Not Explain It

21. The jury would not be authorized to award punitive damages to *W*, because damages for future lost profits suffered by a new enterprise are exceedingly difficult to prove with reasonable certainty, if the court would allow such proof at all.

To create an extreme example from two previous illustrations, imagine that your friend exclaimed, "The sun will definitely rise tomorrow morning, because chocolate cake tastes terrible when covered with spicy tomato sauce." When viewed in isolation, each clause in the sentence is perfectly accurate. However, the conclusion in the opening clause is accurate (in most parts of the world) because of general principles about the rotation of the earth and not because of a presumed distaste for tomato sauce on chocolate cake. The explanation in the second clause is simply irrelevant to the correct conclusion in the first clause.

Similarly, in assertion 21, the conclusion in the opening clause correctly rules out punitive damages for breach of contract, and the second clause accurately summarizes the difficulty of proving lost profits suffered by a new enterprise without a record of past profits, even under a liberal standard that would allow such proof. However, the two clauses in the assertion are totally unrelated to each other in subject matter: One addresses punitive damages and the other addresses compensatory damages for consequential losses in the form of lost profits. The conclusion in the first clause is correct for a reason other than the explanation offered in the second clause; thus, the clauses are not accurately linked in a causal relationship, as is erroneously asserted by the word *because*.

The clauses would at least be related if the first one were changed to read: "*W* would not be entitled to damages for future lost profits . . . ." Even then, however, the total assertion would be false, because the second clause misstates the facts; the problem posits that *W*'s factory is "established and profitable" rather than a new enterprise.

6. Exercise: Five True–False Questions Relating to Common Facts

Questions 1-5. The five true–false questions below all relate to the following facts.

This set of questions addresses punitive damages, which are damages that go beyond compensating for actual loss and are designed to punish bad behavior and to discourage such behavior in future cases. This section does not assume that you have studied anything about punitive damages. The fact pattern and the claim are simply a context within which to ask you some questions about legal method. You may assume that no state constitutional or statutory provisions apply to this issue, until legislation is proposed or assumed in question 5 below.

Let's examine the imaginary case of *Smith v. Jones* (1906). In that case, let's imagine that the Arizona Supreme Court decided as a matter of common law that a jury may award punitive damages for one party's breach of an oral contract between two parties to marry one another. This is an exceptional decision, because, although punitive damages are often awarded for serious "torts," many cases before and since *Smith v. Jones* have established that punitive damages are not awarded in Arizona for breach of any kind of contract, other than a contract to marry. In *Smith v. Jones*, the Arizona Supreme Court reasoned that breach of a contract to marry may injure the honor of the family of the victim of the breach, possibly leading to destructive retaliation against the breaching party unless punitive damages are available. One hundred years later, in the lawsuit of *Aranda v. Wells* (2006), the victim of a breach of an oral contract to marry seeks compensatory and punitive damages.

In another case arising in Arizona, *Wang v. Kay*, a surrogate mother breached her surrogacy contract and refused to relinquish custody of the baby that she had carried to full term, and the couple who supplied the fertilized egg have sued the surrogate mother for compensatory and punitive damages for breach of the surrogacy contract. Yet another case arising in California, *Soto v. Hutchison*, is identical to *Aranda v. Wells*.

1. T _____ F _____ In *Aranda v. Wells*, if the trial court and the intermediate court of appeals in Arizona believe that the reasoning and rule of *Smith v. Jones* are no longer consistent with modern social values,

they may ignore that precedent, even if *Smith v. Jones* has never been overruled.

2. T _____ F _____ In *Soto v. Hutchison*, if the trial court and the intermediate court of appeals in California are not persuaded by the reasoning of *Smith v. Jones*, they may ignore that Arizona precedent, even if *Smith v. Jones* has never been overruled.

3. T _____ F _____ In *Wang v. Kay*, if any of the state courts wants to deny punitive damages for breach of the surrogacy contract, it can distinguish *Smith v. Jones* and thereby reach a different conclusion than that of *Smith v. Jones* without overruling it.

4. T _____ F _____ When *Aranda v. Wells* reaches the Arizona Supreme Court, a majority of justices of that court view *Smith v. Jones* as outdated, but they have no authority to overrule that precedent, because only the legislature can modify or overrule the common law precedent of *Smith v. Jones*.

5. T _____ F _____ If the Arizona Supreme Court in *Aranda v. Wells* retains the rule allowing punitive damages for breach of a contract to marry, reaffirming *Smith v. Jones*, the state legislature can overrule this long-standing rule of state common law by enacting a statute that limits damages for such contracts to certain kinds of compensatory damages.

D. Summary

The illustrations of false assertions in this discussion of true–false questions likely do not address every type of flaw that can render an assertion false for purposes of a true–false test. However, they serve to educate you about the process of critical and even skeptical reading that you will apply in such an exam. If you have come this far, you know nearly all you need to know about multiple-choice questions as well.

III. MULTIPLE-CHOICE QUESTIONS

A. Relationship to True–False Questions

If you skipped over the discussion of true–false questions in the last section, thinking that you were interested only in multiple-choice questions, you should return to the beginning of this chapter. You will soon find that each multiple-choice question is essentially a collection of true–false questions, all but one of which are false (or, much less commonly, all but one of which are true).

Professors probably find it easier to draft challenging true–false questions if the assertions are false. They can test the depth of your knowledge and analytic abilities by hiding subtle flaws in statements that appear to be accurate at first glance. True statements probably are not equally effective tools for exposing gaps in a student's knowledge. Consequently, multiple-choice questions are more attractive to most professors than are true–false questions, because they permit a predictable pattern of three to four false assertions for every one correct assertion.

B. Fundamental Strategies

The typical multiple-choice question will provide you with four or five alternative assertions and will invite you to select the single assertion that is correct. Your task is to examine each assertion, read it carefully and critically (as you would a true–false question), and eliminate it from consideration if it is false.

In this manner, you frequently will be able to eliminate all but two assertions as clearly false, with the two remaining assertions competing for your selection as the single correct response. At this point, you will want to hold an analytic magnifying glass to each remaining assertion, searching for a flaw such as those discussed in Section II of this chapter. If you find a flaw in one but not the other, you can eliminate the remaining inaccurate assertion, leaving the correct answer.

You can achieve the same result by affirmatively looking for the single response that is correct, based on which response is most appealing. Although this positive approach might reap quick rewards on easy questions, it might be insufficiently critical in nature to easily identify the single correct answer on more difficult questions. On challenging questions, this positive approach might lead you to identify all, or nearly all, the assertions as correct.

Instead, you should seek to unmask the cleverly written false assertions and test the accuracy of the single correct one. You can accomplish this most effectively by actively searching for flaws in each assertion, with the goal of proving each assertion to be false. If all goes well, only one assertion will survive your scrutiny.

C. Forms of Multiple-Choice Questions

1. Alternative Abstract Statements of the Law

Like the true–false questions discussed earlier, a multiple-choice question might present an abstract assertion of law, with little introductory material, or it might set forth a fact pattern followed by assertions that apply law to facts to reach a conclusion. A question of the first type, for example, might introduce four or five assertions of law with the following query: "Which of the following is the best statement of the law regarding defenses to a tort claim for negligence?"

2. Fact-Based Questions

The second type, based on a fact pattern, would look very much like the illustration in Section II.C, except that one, and only one, alternative response would be true.

> 17. *W* entered into a contract with *B* in which *B* agreed for a fee to supply water from *B*'s well to *W*'s established and profitable but remote factory. *B* knew that *W*'s factory would cease operating if the water supply were interrupted. After performing the contract without incident for one month, a feud developed between *W* and *B*, and *B* intentionally cut off the flow of water to *W*'s factory for the purpose of causing *W* to suffer economic losses. In a lawsuit, *W* proved with certainty that *B* intentionally breached the contract without excuse, causing *W* to suffer losses, including lost profits, but *W* did not prove facts supporting any tort or other type of claim. Thus, remedies must be based solely on the claim for breach of contract, and the contract does not address remedies for breach. Which of the following statements represents the best analysis of the law and the facts in most states?
>
> A. *W* cannot recover damages for lost profits, because compensatory damages are awarded for unavoidable, foreseeable losses that *W* proves with reasonable certainty, but not including lost profits, even if they are proved under those standards.
> B. The court would not authorize the jury to award damages for emotional distress, because no state's law permits such damages for breach of contract in any circumstances.
> C. The court would not authorize the jury to award punitive damages to *W*, because the contract did not include a clause in which the parties agreed that the victim of breach would be entitled to punitive damages in addition to compensation for actual losses.
> D. *W* would not be entitled to damages for the emotional distress that he suffered as a result of the breach, because in most states such damages cannot be recovered only for breach of a contract designed to protect emotional sensibilities or for breaches that cause personal injury.
> E. The jury would not be authorized to award punitive damages to *W*, because damages for future lost profits suffered by a new enterprise are exceedingly difficult to prove with reasonable certainty, if the court would allow such proof at all.

For the reasons stated in Section II.C, all of these assertions are inaccurate, except for assertion D, which I have altered here to make it the single true answer.

Some professors tend to follow a special pattern in fact-based, multiple-choice questions. They present four alternative assertions, two of which state the same conclusion but with different supporting arguments, and the other two of which state the other conclusion, each with a different supporting argument. Using a fact pattern that is slightly modified from that just set forth, a question of this type might look like the following:

17. *W* entered into a contract with *B* in which *B* agreed for a fee to supply water from *B*'s well to *W*'s established and profitable but remote factory. *B* knew that *W*'s factory would cease operating if the water supply were interrupted. After performing the contract without incident for one month, a feud developed between *W* and *B*, and *B* intentionally cut off the flow of water to *W*'s factory for the purpose of causing *W* to suffer economic losses. In a lawsuit, *W* proved with certainty that *B* intentionally breached the contract without excuse, causing *W* to suffer losses, including lost profits, but *W* did not prove facts supporting any tort or other type of claim. Thus, remedies must be based solely on the claim for breach of contract. Which of the following statements represents the best analysis of the law and the facts in most states?

A. The jury could exercise discretion to award punitive damages to *W*, because *B* breached the contract intentionally, for the purpose of causing *W* to suffer losses.
B. The jury could exercise discretion to award punitive damages to *W*, but only if the contract included a clause in which the parties agreed that the victim of breach would be entitled to punitive damages in addition to compensation for actual losses.
C. The jury would not be authorized to award punitive damages to *W*, because the law in most states will not permit punitive damages for even an intentional breach of contract, and will not enforce a contractual penalty clause.
D. The jury would not be authorized to award punitive damages to *W*, because damages for future lost profits suffered by a new enterprise are exceedingly difficult to prove with reasonable certainty, if the court would allow such proof at all.

As discussed earlier, the first two assertions are incorrect because the law of most states will not authorize an award of punitive damages for breach of contract, nor will it enforce a contractual penalty clause. Thus, the opening conclusions of assertions A and B immediately reveal their falsity. Assertion C is the opposite of the combined assertions A and B, and it states the correct conclusion and the correct legal premises. Assertion D states the correct conclusion but supports the conclusion with a legal standard that is irrelevant to punitive damages and with an incorrect factual characterization of the factory as a new enterprise.

Note that this illustration includes a new kind of assertion, one that introduces a hypothetical factual premise. For this example, I omitted mention in the fact statement of the absence of contractual damages clause, allowing assertion B to condition its conclusion on the presence of a penalty clause. This technique allows greater variability in the assertions but does not change the nature of your task.

3. Explain the Answer

A few professors ask students not only to identify the single correct response (or, less commonly, the single incorrect response), but also to explain in a sentence or two why each alternative response is either correct or incorrect. I would characterize such a question as a combination multiple-choice question and a short-answer essay question.

If you analyze each assertion in the multiple-choice question in the critical manner recommended in this chapter, rather than simply reacting intuitively, you should have no problem writing your explanations. For most assertions, you will simply articulate the critical thought process that led you to reject the assertion as false or flawed. Borrowing from an earlier illustration in Section II.C.3, you might explain, for example, that "Answer C is flawed because, although it correctly excludes punitive damages, it incorrectly assumes that the conclusion would be different if the parties had agreed to a penalty clause; such a clause would be unenforceable as a violation of public policy."

You normally can explain the correct assertion by simply pointing out the absence of any flaws: "Answer D is correct because it correctly states the stringent standard for awarding damages for emotional distress in a contract claim, and it correctly concludes that the standard would not be satisfied in the breach of an ordinary commercial contract."

IV. AMBIGUITY OR ERRORS IN OBJECTIVE QUESTIONS

A. The Nature of the Problem

If your professor replaces half of an essay exam with objective questions, he or she can cover a broad range of issues while halving his or her burden of reading and evaluating essay answers. Good objective questions, however, are exceedingly difficult to write.

Unlike essay questions, which typically are designed to encourage discussion of arguments for both sides of a dispute, an assertion in an objective question must be unambiguously true or false. When a professor focuses largely on eliminating ambiguities from an assertion, however, the truth or falsity of the assertion tends to stand out too obviously, resulting in a relatively easy question that does not help the professor distinguish between students who know the law with impressive depth and specificity and those who are only moderately well prepared. When a professor focuses largely on writing a question that challenges even the best students, however, the difficulty of ensuring a single unambiguously correct answer increases.

Consequently, you might occasionally encounter an objective question that is poorly designed in one of the following ways: (1) the question contains an apparent mistake or omission, (2) two or more assertions in a multiple-choice question are equally correct, or (3) no assertion is entirely correct. For example, you might find that an assertion contains a tiny flaw that arguably makes it false, but you believe that the professor did not notice the minuscule flaw and intended the assertion to be true.

A responsible professor will do everything possible to eliminate such questions before the exam is given, or will score the exams without counting such questions if the professor learns of the flaws immediately after the exam is given. You should be prepared, however, to react appropriately when you encounter a question that you believe is flawed in its design.

B. Reacting to Mistakes or Flaws in an Objective Question

Some professors explicitly permit you to write comments in the question booklet about errors or ambiguities in questions. If your professor, however, deducts points for poorly reasoned comments, do not lightly comment on a question.

In my experience, at least 75 percent of student comments written on my multiple-choice exam booklets and directed to my attention display confusion about the law or about the proper application of the law to the facts. Very few reveal a problem with the question. If the students marked the correct answer, I give them full credit despite any confusion displayed in their comments. However, if your professor announces that he or she gives no credit for correct answers when accompanied by poor explanations volunteered by a student, you should look very hard for the correct answer before concluding and commenting that the question itself is flawed.

On rare occasions, however, a comment will persuade me that a student fully understood the law and the facts, even though the student marked the answer that I deemed to be wrong. On those occasions, I give the student full or partial credit, as the circumstances dictate.

Every now and then, a student comment will persuade me that a multiple-choice question contains an error or is poorly designed, perhaps because two alternative assertions are as equally valid as the correct answer. If so, I will give credit to any student who selected either of the correct answers, or I will toss the question out and ignore it in the scoring.

In sum, I believe you can draw the following lessons from these observations. If your professor invites you to comment on the validity of objective questions and does not penalize you for making a poorly reasoned comment, you should not hesitate to add a comment if you have good reason to conclude that a question is flawed and if you have enough time for both the comment and the remaining questions. On the other hand, if your professor invites comments but exacts some sort of penalty for poorly reasoned comments, you should add a comment only if you are confident of your analysis and are certain, after scrutinizing it carefully, that the question is flawed.

If your professor has made no provision for commentary on questions that are arguably flawed, you can safely assume that he or she will not deduct points for a commentary, even if it strikes the professor as poorly reasoned. However, it is also likely that the professor does not intend to read the question booklet and look for sound and helpful commentary. Therefore, if you believe that a question is flawed, you can describe the flaw in the question booklet or on scratch paper, and notify the exam administrator about the problem at the end of the exam period. The exam administrator will likely relay the comment to the professor, who might be open to reassessing the validity of the question.

V. EXERCISES: MULTIPLE CHOICE

A. Theories of Contract Liability

After studying consideration, quasi-contract, promissory estoppel, and moral obligation in your Contracts course, answer the following questions:

1. After a particularly wild New Year's Eve party, Bob and Larry, both adults, met for a game of basketball on January 1. After complaining about their bad habits and discussing New Year's resolutions, Bob stated to Larry: "I promise to quit drinking alcoholic beverages for the rest of this year if you promise to quit smoking cigarettes for the entire year." Larry responded: "Agreed." Which of the following best describes the rights and obligations of the parties?

A. Although a breach may be difficult to remedy, if each sought the other's forbearance in exchange for his own, expressing a serious legal intent, Bob and Larry formed an enforceable contract supported by a bargained-for exchange.

B. Although a breach may be difficult to remedy, Bob and Larry formed an enforceable contract, but only if each party must incur some cost or suffer some other tangible detriment in performing his promise.

C. Although a breach may be difficult to remedy, Bob and Larry formed an enforceable contract, but only if each party will derive some tangible benefit from the other party's performance.

D. Neither Bob nor Larry is contractually bound, because Bob has a legal right to drink alcoholic beverages and Larry has a legal right to smoke.
E. Neither Bob nor Larry is contractually bound, because each gave only an illusory promise to the other.

2. Which of the following most clearly expresses an illusory promise?

A. If you come to my house to pick it up, you can have my TV set. [The speaker doesn't want to be bothered to deliver the TV set, so she is asking that recipient of the statement come to get the set.]
B. I want you to have the choice of quitting your work if you so desire, so I promise to pay you $30,000 a year until your social security payments begin.
C. I will sell you all of the output of computer chips from my plant on Brokaw Ave. for the first six months of the calendar year 2000.
D. If you agree to pay me $100/hour, I will provide you with such consulting services as I desire to make available to you.
E. I promise to forbear from collecting my claim against you for a reasonable time.

3. James worked as the butler for Catherine, a wealthy Beverly Hills socialite, for 20 years in exchange for room, board, and an average salary of $25,000 a year. James retired and moved into his own apartment on October 1. At a gala party on October 5 marking James's retirement, Catherine made the following statement to James and the rest of the celebrants: "James, I am so very grateful for your decades of faithful, expert, and sensitive service that I will buy you a new Lexus sedan to replace that old jalopy of yours. James, just let me know when you want to pick out and drive away your new car, and I will make good on that promise." A few minutes later, James approached Catherine and thanked her for her unexpected generosity. Catherine replied: "I'm sorry James, I made that statement solely to impress my friends. I can't afford to buy you a new car. This party has already cost me plenty. What more do you want?" Which of the following best expresses the rights and obligations of the parties?

A. Catherine is liable to James for breach of contract: By promising to buy a car in exchange for his promise to select a car and drive it away, she proposed a bargained-for exchange, to which he agreed when he thanked her.
B. Catherine is liable to James for breach of contract, based on her moral obligation to James in light of his selfless service over 20 years.
C. Catherine is liable to James on the basis of promissory estoppel; a court would enforce her promise to buy James a new car, or at least would award reliance damages based on the anticipated cost of his having to continue to maintain his current car.

D. Catherine is liable to James on the basis of quasi-contract, because it would be unjust for her not to provide additional compensation for James's decades of selfless service.

E. Catherine may be self-centered and lacking in moral character, but she is not legally liable to James based on her statements at the party.

B. Five Civil Procedure Questions Based on Extensive Common Facts

After you have studied the Federal Rules of Civil Procedure (the "Rules") that focus on pleading, discovery, and resolution prior to trial (Rules 8, 9, 11, 12, 16, 26-37, 41, 55 and 56), you can take this factually rich multiple-choice exam created by Professor Bob Dauber and used here with his permission. You may consult the Rules when you answer these questions.

General Instructions

The Questions on this examination relate to the Basic Facts that follow these General Instructions; some Questions will add facts to the Basic Facts. You should assume that the facts added by each Question apply only to that Question unless otherwise specified.

You should answer all Questions according to the Federal Rules of Civil Procedure, unless the question specifically refers to state court litigation. You may consult the rules of Federal Civil Procedure when you take this exam.

Basic Facts

In 2008, Paula Phish developed a process for converting algae into a very effective organic fertilizer without emitting any greenhouse gas. She started a company, Algor, Inc., to manufacture and market the fertilizer, hiring her college roommate, Donna Draper, to be chief operating officer. While Phish had a chemistry degree, Draper's expertise was in marketing and agribusiness. By 2012, Algor was grossing $20 million/year in sales of its only product, Algi-pellets, and had a manufacturing plant in Tempe, Arizona that employed 20 people, and a second plant in Fresno, California that employed 32 people. Phish's annual income was close to $2 million, while Draper was being paid $250,000/year as Chief Operating Officer under her employment contract with Algor.

In June 2012, Draper approached Phish, seeking an equity interest in the business. Phish refused, and Draper tendered her resignation. Two months later, Phish learned that Draper had moved to California and had become the new Vice President of Fertilife, Inc., a California-based multinational corporation that sold a variety of products to farmers, including nonsynthetic fertilizers for organic farming. Shortly after hiring Draper, Fertilife began aggressively marketing a new algae-based product, "Ferti-pellets," which appeared very similar to Algor's fertilizer. The advertised price of Ferti-pellets was slightly higher than the price of Algi-pellets. Nevertheless, Algor, Inc. experienced an immediate drop in business. Phish soon learned from her former customers that Draper had contacted each of them personally and offered to supply them with Fertilife's product for 10% less than the cost they had been paying for Algi-pellets. Phish tried adjusting the price points for Algi-pellets, but the damage had been done. By the end of the year, Algor's sales were down more than 50 percent, and Phish had to close her Fresno plant and lay off 25 workers.

In early 2013, Phish contacted her lawyer, Larry Liner, to investigate whether she might have any claims against Draper or Fertilife for stealing her product and her business. After reviewing the employment contract Draper had signed when she joined Algor, Liner advised Phish that the contract contained a standard noncompete clause (providing that Draper would not work for a competitor of Algor for a period of five years following any separation of employment) as well as a provision requiring Draper to maintain the confidentiality of any and all of Algor's trade secrets. Liner told Phish that Draper obviously had violated the confidentiality provision by providing Fertilife with the formula for producing Algi-pellets, as well as Algor's customer list and price sheet, and she also had violated the noncompete provision. In addition, Liner concluded that Fertilife is most likely liable to Algor under a tort theory of unfair competition, which imposes liability on a business for misappropriation of a competitor's trade secrets and for intentional interference with a competitor's business relations.

Liner explained to Phish that he could institute a lawsuit against Draper and Fertilife, seeking millions of dollars in compensation for the damage done to Algor, but it will be an expensive proposition, requiring expert testimony and extensive discovery. Liner said he would need an initial retainer of $100,000. Phish agreed and instructed Liner to proceed as quickly as possible. On behalf of Phish's company, Algor, Inc., Liner filed a complaint in federal court, which was personally served on Draper and Fertilife on March 1, 2013.

Multiple-Choice Questions

1. Which of the following is most accurate?

A. Draper and Fertilife have 60 days to respond to the Complaint pursuant to Rule 4(d)(3).

B. Plaintiff may ask the court for a default judgment against Draper and Fertilife if they have not responded to the Complaint by March 22, 2013.

C. Plaintiff may ask the clerk of the court to enter Draper's and Fertilife's default if they have not responded to the Complaint by March 22, 2013.

D. Plaintiff may not seek a default judgment against these defendants because the Complaint seeks relief other than a sum that can be made certain by computation.

E. Draper and Fertilife have approximately 83 days to respond to the Complaint.

2. Assume that Draper and Fertilife both file motions to dismiss pursuant to Rule 12(b)(1) on March 15, 2013, and the Court denies both motions on April 1, 2013. Which of the following is true?

A. If Draper files a subsequent motion to dismiss for improper venue pursuant to Rule 12(b)(3), the Court is likely to deny the motion because Draper failed to consolidate it with her motion to dismiss under Rule 12(b)(1).

B. Draper must file a response to Plaintiff's Complaint by April 15, 2013.

C. The parties' disclosure statements must be exchanged approximately 83 days from March 15, 2013.

D. All of the above.

E. (a) and (b) only.

3. Assume that Fertilife has documents establishing conclusively that it independently developed the formula for Ferti-pellets well before hiring Draper as Vice President. You are counsel for Fertilife. How would you advise your client?

A. Fertilife need not produce copies of the documents unless and until Algor, Inc. asks for them in a Request for Production under Rule 34.

B. Fertilife should voluntarily produce copies of these documents to counsel for Algor, Inc. as part of its initial disclosure.

C. Fertilife may claim that these documents are protected from disclosure based on the work-product doctrine.

D. It would be wise for Fertilife to not produce the documents until trial, so that they may be used to impeach Algor's witnesses.

E. Both (c) and (d) are correct.

4. Counsel for Fertilife wants to take the deposition of Paula Phish. Which of the following is most accurate?

A. Phish may not be deposed because she is not a party to the lawsuit.

B. Phish may be deposed any time after Fertilife responds to the Complaint, provided that Phish is served with a subpoena under Rule 45.

C. Phish may not be deposed until after the parties have exchanged their disclosure statements.

D. Fertilife's lawyer may serve Phish with interrogatories to answer under oath if she does not want to pay for a deposition.

E. Both (b) and (d) are accurate.

5. After filing an Answer to the Complaint denying liability, Tom Herrera, the attorney for Fertilife, Inc., spent days combing through Fertilife's electronic communications and learned that Fertilife's president sent Draper an e-mail on May 28, 2007, offering Draper a $1 million signing bonus if she were to "join Fertilife's management team" and provide Fertilife with the formula for Algi-pellets. Which of the following is **NOT** true?

A. Fertilife is not required to produce a copy of this e-mail as part of its initial disclosure under Rule 26(a) because it is damaging to Fertilife's case.

B. If this case were pending in Arizona state court, instead of federal court, Fertilife would be required to disclose this e-mail to Algor, Inc. under Rule 26.1 of the Arizona Rules of Civil Procedure.

C. Herrera may be subject to sanctions under Rule 11 if he continues to advocate in court that Fertilife did not engage in unfair competition.

D. The e-mail is protected from disclosure and discovery under the attorney work-product doctrine.

E. If Algor serves Fertilife with a request for production of documents seeking "all written and electronic correspondence between Draper and Fertilife while Draper was still employed by Algor, Inc.," Fertilife will be required to produce a copy of this e-mail to Algor, Inc.

VI. THE NEXT STEP

In the best of all worlds, you have completed this book before your first day of law school. Armed with a clear picture of your destination and with a map of the road ahead, you are ready to take the necessary steps throughout the semester that will enable you to perform your best on final exams.

In particular, remember a few key points:

- Steady and diligent work throughout the semester—including in your Legal Writing class—will pay great dividends at exam time.
- Know your audience. Take steps to determine the style of exams that your professors tend to give and the kinds of responses they prefer.
- Practice makes perfect. Take as many practice or past exams as you can.
- Maintain a healthy perspective and take steps to control stress.
- Take your exams with confidence and with effective exam techniques.

Good luck, work hard, and enjoy the journey.

Epilogue

If you study hard throughout the semester but do not score as highly as you had hoped on your first set of exams, do not despair, and do not withdraw from active class participation in the second semester. After all, it would be difficult indeed to maintain the same class standing that you enjoyed in college, because your law school class is entirely composed of exceptional students who—like you—graduated near the top of their college classes. Instead, you might react constructively in one of several ways.

If your first semester or first year of law school is a complete disaster, you might well conclude that law is not your best career choice. If so, do not denigrate yourself or your talents. Aptitude for the study of law is not a measure of your worth as a human being or your capability of contributing to society in equally or more important ways.

If your initial exam scores are greatly disappointing but you are determined to pursue a career in law, remember that many law students who graduate with low grade point averages ultimately become very successful attorneys, even though their initial employment options are more limited. So, keep your spirits up, and take steps to continually improve your grades. At the least, review your exams and any model answers released by your professors, and visit with your professors to obtain further advice, so that you can identify the weaknesses in your performance and take steps to address them. If you are eligible for assistance in an Academic Success Program at your school, avail yourself of that opportunity. You might also benefit from reading this book again, from cover to cover. The information in it likely will be more meaningful after you have had some experience with the facets of legal education that it addresses.

Finally, if you succeed in earning high grades on law school exams, congratulations. Those grades represent the acquisition of knowledge and analytic skills that will serve you well in practice, particularly if combined with other qualities and skills that cannot so easily be taught and examined in law school. The high grades will increase your options for postgraduate employment, but you should not necessarily be seduced by the highest salary that is offered to you. You have worked hard to develop marketable skills. Take some time and effort to determine what kind of practice will best help you achieve a sense of satisfaction in your career and overall happiness in your life.

Here's wishing you success in law school, a satisfying career, and a full and happy life.

Sample Answers to Outlining Exercises in Chapter 6, Section V

A. Outlining: Ads as Offers

IV. Offer—An offer is an expression reasonably understood as a commitment to enter into a contract on definite terms, empowering the offeree to create a contract by agreeing.

. . . .

D. Ads: Under the common law, a seller's ad to sell goods at a certain price is reasonably interpreted only as an invitation to submit offers unless it is so definite that it expresses commitment and leaves nothing important left to negotiate.

1. Example: In *Craft*, a general ad stating the price for a certain model sewing machine was not an offer, partly because it did not limit the quantity for sale and identify who could accept, so that a reasonable reader would not conclude that the seller was ready to commit.

2. Example: In *Lefkowitz*, an ad for a single fur stole to be sold "first-come, first-served," was reasonably interpreted as an offer, expressing the seller's commitment to a deal, because it limited the seller's potential obligation to a defined quantity and to a defined offeree.

3. Comment: Because most newspaper advertisements are as general as that in *Craft*, some authorities state a general rule that newspaper advertisements are not offers absent "special circumstances."

B. Outlining: Consideration

I. Consideration is a bargained-for exchange in which a party exchanges a promise for either a promise or a completed performance. It is not satisfied by a promise to make a gift to another.

A. Elements of Exchange—Performance and Promises

1. Performances—A performance can be an act, forbearance, or change in legal relationship, and it can be exchanged as consideration regardless whether the performing party suffers any tangible detriment in performing.

a. Acts—Typical acts that qualify as performances are payment of money, delivery of goods, transfer of title, or provision of services.

i. Example: In *Hamer v. Sidway*, the act of paying money was assumed to be a valid performance that could be promised.

ii. Example: In *Kirksey v. Kirksey*, Antillico's act of moving her household 60 miles presumably could be a valid performance; consequently, the majority's finding no consideration must rest on other grounds if contemporary standards apply.

b. Forbearances—A forbearance from engaging in a lawful act or from asserting a legal right is a valid performance.

i. Example: In *Hamer*, the nephew's forbearing from participating in legal activities, such as swearing and using tobacco, was a valid performance, regardless whether the abstentions were difficult for the nephew or benefitted him rather than caused him a detriment.

ii. Example: In *Fiege v. Boehm*, Hilda's forbearance from asserting her statutory paternity claim against Louis (in exchange for his promise of support) was a valid forbearance so long as they had a good-faith belief in the validity of her claim when they contracted, even if her claim turned out to be factually groundless because another man was the father.

2. Promises—A promise of a future performance can be exchanged as consideration, but it must state a commitment, subject only to events not entirely within the promisor's control, rather than leaving performance or withdrawal entirely to the promisor's unrestricted discretion and whim.

a. Example from hypo: The insurer of a home likely will never pay a penny on its promise, but its promise to pay in the event of a covered loss is subject to a condition outside its control, so its promise is a good commitment and is not illusory.

b. Example: In *Strong v. Sheffield*, a promise to forbear from collecting a debt until the creditor "wants" the money was illusory because it was interpreted to mean that the creditor could either forbear or not at his own whim.

c. Example: In *Wood v. Lucy, Lady Duff-Gordon*, Wood had not clearly expressed a promise to do more than solicit sales of Lucy's fashions if he felt like doing so, but the court found a minimum commitment on his part to use reasonable efforts, implied from various terms and recitals in the contract.

d. Example: Even a promise that is subject to a condition of subjective satisfaction with the other party's performance is valid and non-illusory, because the promisor must review the work and determine in good faith (honestly) whether the performance meets the promisor's personal standards and must perform on the promise if those standards are satisfied.

B. Bargained-for: Reciprocal Inducement—A promise for a promise, or a promise for a performance, is a bargained-for exchange only if each party genuinely seeks the other's promise or performance, in a current exchange.

    1. Example: In *Kirksey*, the majority decision can be explained by a finding that the brother-in-law was not seeking Antillico's moving to his estate in exchange for his promise to provide her a place to stay; rather than inducement to him, her moving was simply a necessary condition to her accepting his promised gift of a place to stay.

    2. Example: If a purported consideration is so insignificant that it is no genuine inducement at all for the recipient, then the purported exchange lacks reciprocal inducement and likely is a promised gift dressed up to look like an exchange.

    3. Example: If one gives a promise in recognition of a past performance, it lacks reciprocal inducement, because the past performance could not have been induced by a promise that did not yet exist, and the promise and performance are not part of a current exchange.

C. Moral Obligation Theory—Notwithstanding the failure of a past performance to constitute consideration for a subsequent promise (see above), some courts will nonetheless enforce the subsequent promise if made in recognition of a moral obligation arising out of the past performance.

    1. Example: In *Webb v. McGowin*, the court enforced a promise by an employer to pay a stipend to an employee who suffered permanent injuries when saving the employer from death or serious injury in a workplace accident.

    2. Example: In *Harrington v. Taylor*, however, a court denied enforcement of a man's subsequent promise to pay on equally compelling facts, when a neighbor saved the man from death or serious injury by deflecting an axe being wielded against him, suffering permanent injuries to her hand.

    3. Explanation: In *Mills v. Wyman*, the court rejected moral obligation theory to preserve predictability and certainty in the law, even at the expense of justice in some cases, suggesting that it would be difficult to predict when a fact-finder would find that a past performance gave rise to a moral obligation.

Sample Answers to Essay Exam Exercises in Chapter 10, Section IV

A. A Nonlegal Setting

1. Did Lina return "home" by midnight on Friday night?

With exceptions that do not apply to the Friday night date, Lina must return from social outings by midnight. *See* Case #2; Case #3. It's not clear how that rule applies to this case, because Lina returned to the driveway of her home by 11:55 P.M., within the curfew, but did not enter her home until 12:15 A.M., fifteen minutes beyond the curfew.

On these facts, Lina might have satisfied the curfew, because Lina has technically returned home before midnight by returning to the family property, albeit outside the house. One of the policy concerns underlying the curfew rule is Lina's safe return at night. That policy is likely to be vindicated if Lina has safely returned to the general property by midnight and is appropriately socializing within her mother's view. A focus on that policy, therefore, supports a liberal interpretation of the rule that would find no violation in this case.

On the other hand, the policy of promoting health and adequate time for sleep is not advanced by Lina's presence in the driveway, because Lina cannot prepare to sleep until she enters the house. If the curfew rule is accordingly interpreted to require Lina to enter the house before midnight, this case is not materially distinguishable from Case 3, in which Lina was admonished for returning home after midnight after football and pizza.

I conclude that . . . . [Either conclusion is fine.]

2. Does the basketball game qualify as an exception to curfew rule?

The curfew rule does not apply to important family events, such as the wedding of a relative, particularly if Lina's mother is present at the event. *See* Case #4. In this case, Lina wishes to watch Lina's brother play in a basketball game, an event that arguably is a significant family event justifying an exception to the curfew rule.

An exception might be appropriate, because Lina is obviously closely related to her brother, and the first game of the season likely is an important event for the brother and thus for Lina's family. Moreover, particularly because Lina's mother will not attend this game, Lina's brother will not receive any family support unless Lina attends.

On the other hand, the absence of Lina's mother at the first game suggests that, unlike a relative's wedding, the game is not a significant family event; it is one of more than two dozen in the season, which will include home games that are more convenient for the family to attend. Moreover, a family event justifies an exception to the curfew rule partly because the mother is present to monitor the activities of her children. Even if Lina's brother strongly desires support from some family member at the first game of the season, Lina's attending the game alone would not satisfy her mother's desire to monitor her activities after midnight. This factor is mitigated, but perhaps not eliminated, by the fact that Lina would travel to the away game with another family.

On balance, I conclude . . . . [Either conclusion is fine.]

B. Samaritan's Tort Liability for Rose's Injuries

Vicarious Liability—Samaritan will be vicariously liable for the negligence of its employees for actions taken during the course of their employment. The injuries in this case grew out of actions taken by Kelly, an anesthesiologist employed and paid a salary by Samaritan, and assigned by Samaritan to Rose's surgery. Thus, Samaritan will be liable for Kelly's negligence during the anesthesiology procedure.

Negligence—Negligence is a breach of duty of care owed to another, proximately causing injuries, and in the absence of a defense such as assumption of the risk.

Breach of Duty of Care—Kelly owed to Rose a duty to exercise at least the ordinary skill and care that is customary among anesthesiologists in the state.

In this case, Kelly was careful to inform Rose of the risks and benefits of the alternative types of general anesthesia, allowing her to make an informed choice. Nothing in the facts suggests that Kelly or anyone else in the hospital was careless in failing to discover Rose's rare condition. Moreover, Kelly carefully focused on the intake gauge during the procedure, in an obvious effort to avoid administering an overdose or administering the substance at an overly rapid rate. Finally, Kelly was sufficiently aware of Rose's condition to cease the administration of anesthesia within a mere ten seconds of her experiencing an adverse reaction.

On the other hand, a hospital's own protocols likely would be good evidence of procedures and standards of care that are customary in the state for administration of anesthesia. Those protocols were violated when

Kelly administered the anesthesia without assistance. Consequently, Kelly's very act of focusing solely on the intake gauge meant that Kelly carelessly took her attention away from other important means of monitoring Rose's reactions. Ten seconds was a very long time for Kelly to be unaware of Rose's reactions in such circumstances, as suggested by the permanent brain damage Rose ultimately sustained.

On balance, I conclude that Kelly was negligent.

Proximate Cause—Although Kelly's actions were a cause in fact of Rose's injuries, neither Kelly nor Samaritan will be liable unless the nexus between Kelly's acts and the injuries is sufficiently close that it makes sense as a policy matter to find liability. This requirement, known as proximate cause, can be undermined by a supervening cause that is more dominant than the negligent act in causing the injuries. However, a tortfeasor must take his victims as he finds them, including being responsible for their unusual susceptibility to injury if liability is otherwise established.

In this case, Samaritan might argue that Rose's rare and undiagnosed condition was a supervening cause that was primarily responsible for the unusual reaction to the generally safe anesthesia. Once that condition triggered the adverse reaction, it's possible that Rose would have suffered the same heart stoppage and consequent injuries even if Kelly had stopped the intake within one second rather than ten.

On the other hand, had Kelly not carelessly administered the anesthesia alone while focusing solely on the intake gauge, Rose at least would have had a greater chance of avoiding the heart stoppage or of having her heartbeat restored in time to prevent brain damage. Moreover, the supervening cause rule should not apply in this context, because Rose's condition is best characterized not as an intervening event, but as a greater susceptibility on her part to sustain injury, the full extent for which the tortfeasor should be liable.

On balance, I conclude that Rose's condition was not a supervening cause and that Kelly's carelessness was a proximate cause of Rose's injuries.

Assumption of the Risk—Samaritan will nonetheless escape liability if Rose knowingly and voluntarily assumed the risk of the adverse reaction to the administration of anesthesia.

Samaritan might argue that Rose assumed the risk of injury by personally choosing ethane, on the basis of its lower cost, after being informed of the relative costs and benefits of alternative forms of anesthesia. Because her injuries resulted from her reaction to ethane, she assumed the very risk that caused her injuries.

On the other hand, Rose did not know of her condition and so did not appreciate the full extent of the risk when she chose ethane. Moreover, she is even less likely to have assumed the risk that Kelly would administer the anesthesia alone and thus make it more difficult to monitor her reactions. Even if she had understood the risks entailed in Kelly's administering anesthesia without assistance, her failure to leave the room as she was being prepped for surgery or to order Kelly to summon assistance would not be viewed as a voluntary assumption of the risks in the circumstances. A patient being prepped for surgery understandably places her trust in the hands of the medical specialists, so her failure to protest or to otherwise assert herself should not be viewed as an implicit assumption of the risk.

On balance, I conclude . . . .

C. Offer: Application of Contract Law to Facts

An offer is an expression reasonably understood as a commitment to enter into a contract on definite terms, empowering the offeree to create a contract by agreeing. Under the common law, a seller's ad to sell goods at a certain price is reasonably interpreted only as an invitation to submit offers unless it is so definite that it expresses commitment and leaves nothing important left to negotiate.

The newspaper ad has some elements of definiteness because it describes the ad PC by model name and number, states the price for a limited three-day period, and even protects the seller from an order of unlimited size by limiting sales to one per customer. Perhaps some readers would conclude that the seller is confident of its ability to fill all such orders made within that limited time period and thus is committing itself. However, the ad does not limit the number of customers who could purchase one ad PC, so it's almost certainly unreasonable to interpret this to be an offer to sell one item each to an indeterminate number of customers, which might result in seller being unable to perform some of the contracts formed. This likely would be viewed under common law as only an invitation to negotiate.

In contrast, the display at the store not only includes information from the ad, it also displays the actual item, and the stock on the shelves, rather than just a depiction of a representative item. True, customers might assume that the stock on the shelves did not represent a quantity limitation, because of an undisclosed amount of stock in the back, and it might then be unreasonable to assume that the store was committing itself to sell to every consumer who saw the display and who assumed more stock in the back. However, it's more reasonable to interpret the display as stating a commitment to sell the computers that are stocked on the shelves and are visible to consumers who have entered the store. A customer who arrives in time to actually pick up a box remaining on the shelf and put it in her shopping cart could conclude that the store is offering that item for sale and is inviting acceptance by taking the item to the check-out counter, and that the offer terminates when no computers are left in the display. By thus protecting the store from potentially unlimited liability, the display in the store is likely to be an offer to any customer who sees a PC remaining in stock and is in position to claim it.

D. Contract Formation: Application of Contract Law to Facts

Acceptance

An acceptance is a manifestation of agreement to the terms of the offer so as to exercise the power to create a contract through assent.

Authorized Mode of Acceptance

The offeror is the master of the offer and can specify a required means of acceptance if she conveys such a restriction clearly. Otherwise, any reasonable means of acceptance will suffice.

As master of the offer, JP arguably has provided that DL can accept only by "signing and returning" the letter, which DL has not yet accomplished on the facts provided. By stating that DL "can accept" by returning the letter, JP suggests that DL cannot accept in any other way.

On the other hand, JP's statement that "you can accept," should be interpreted to mean that signing and returning the letter was a clearly authorized means of acceptance, and likely the strongly preferred one, but not necessarily the only one. To clearly restrict acceptance, JP should have said, "you can accept only by . . . ." or "to accept, you must . . . ."

On balance, I conclude . . . .

Unambiguous Notice of Acceptance

An acceptance must unequivocally and unambiguously express assent to the offer, so that a reasonable person would believe that the offeree is excercising the power to create a contract by agreeing to the offer.

Even if another means of acceptance is permitted, DL's conduct of sending an employee to secure soil samples is ambiguous: perhaps DL is having second thoughts and wants to study the soil to determine whether its $100,000 bid is sufficient to enable it to perform up to JP's newly defined, very demanding standards. Moreover, JP did not waive notice of acceptance, and is not even at home to witness this conduct, so it is not directly communicated to her, which also amplifies any ambiguity and hampers clarification.

On the other hand, by sending a foreman to JP's house to collect soil samples to facilitate performance, DL arguably has accepted JP's counter-offer through expressive conduct that conveys its return promise to perform the obligations outlined in JP's letter. That interpretation of DL's actions on Oct. 10 is particularly reasonable when its conduct is viewed in light of DL's earlier having submitted a bid to perform the work at the price stated in JP's letter, which was based on detailed specifications. A reasonable person could conclude that DL sent a foreman to collect a soil sample because it was intending to accept the offer and desired to be in a good position to meet JP's performance deadlines and her demanding standards for quality. Although JP is not home to witness this action by DL, the events are relayed to JP through a long-time housekeeper, who presumably is a reliable source. So, through analogy to communication of a revocation through a reliable third party, the housekeeper's call to JP should be viewed as a clear and reliable communication of DL's acceptance.

On balance, I conclude . . . .

Consideration—Illusory Promise

Consideration requires a baragined-for exchange, in which a promise is exchanged for a performance or another promise, with reciprocal inducement. A valid promise expresses commitment, subject only to events not entirely within the promisor's control. On the other hand, if the purported promise leaves the promisor with the option to perform or not, at her own unrestricted discretion, then the purported promise is illusory and does not satisfy the consideration requirement.

Even if DL accepted JP's offer, the parties may have agreed to a transaction without consideration. JP has arguably given an illusory promise, which means that any promise by DL would be gratuitous. JP has not only conditioned her payment obligations on satisfactory completion of a phase of construction according to her "personal standards," she says that approval will be in her "sole judgment." If "sole judgment" is interpreted to mean that JP's evaluations are not tied to any fixed or discernable standards, then her purported promise may be the equivalent of saying "I will pay you if I feel like it," leaving her unfettered discretion whether to perform.

On the other hand, even if JP has conditioned her payment obligation on the exercise of her sole judgment in applying a standard of satisfaction, one can reasonably interpret her statement to identify a real and discernable standard. She stated that her standard relates to quality consistent with her entertaining in a manner befitting the owner of an art gallery, which arguably suggests an objective standard defined by norms in an industry or circle of peers. Frankly, her additional reference to her own "personal standards" strongly favors a subjective standard of satisfaction, but even a subjective standard of satisfaction can bind the promisor. JP may have an unusually high subjective standard for artistic quality, one that surpasses the demands of an objective standard in the industry, but her standard can nonetheless be defined in relation to her desire to impress her peers when entertaining or conducting business, and whether

DL meets that standard is not within JP's control. JP's statement that she is the sole judge of quality makes this a closer case, but that may be interpreted to mean only that JP will be the one to apply her standard, and not some third party such as the company that designed her plans. Her statement still should be interpreted to require her to inspect the work, assess it honestly under her personal standards, and to approve it if DL in fact met her personal standards for excellence.

On balance, I conclude . . . .

E. Unconscionability: Application of Contract Law to Facts

Even if a contract is supported by consideration and not subject to defenses such as duress, fraud, or mutual mistake, a court may deny enforcement if the contract or any part of it is unconscionable. Most states require proof of two branches of this doctrine: (1) procedural unconscionability, which relates to notice of provisions and ability to read, understand, or negotiate the terms, and (2) substantive unconscionability, which refers to oppressive or lopsided terms in the contract.

Several facts support an argument for both procedural and substantive unconscionability.

Procedural: Bill can argue that he lacked meaningful choice. He did not go shopping for a roof treatment but was surprised at home by a door-to-door salesman who applied aggressive sales techniques to get Bill to sign the contract quickly: when Bill stated a desire to compare BB's terms with those of other companies, Jake pressured him to sign right away, before Jake left in the next minute; indeed, Bill apparently felt the need to sign so quickly that he didn't even read the contract he signed, which would have taken a few minutes in light of the relatively small, single-spaced print on the page. Even had he read the contract, which was drafted entirely by BB, it's not clear that Bill would have understood the description of the treatment, which was not high quality. Finally, Jake misleadingly suggested that BB's terms were better than those of other companies, by saying that "we are the best in the business," and by stating that he was "crazy" to lower the price to $4,500. Although this opinion-based "sales puffing" does not constitute misrepresentation, it does constitute a sharp practice in bargaining, contributing to procedural problems.

Substantive: In comparison to terms advertised by other companies in the area, BB's terms were lopsided in favor BB. Unlike other companies, BB did not offer any warranty on the treatment, and its price was significantly higher—more than twice as high in some cases—even though BB offered treatments that were on the lower end of quality. The effective price was higher still, because BB required payment in advance, rather than over two or three months after the work, as permitted by other companies.

On the other hand, BB can argue that the contract is not unconscionable:

Procedural: Although the contract was a form contract, the facts do not show that it was a non-negotiable adhesion contract. Indeed, when Bill hesitated, Jake quickly lowered his price by $500. This suggests that Bill might have successfully bargained for an even lower price, or maybe even a warranty, had to tried to negotiate. The print was small, but it covered only a single page, and it wasn't so small as to be illegible, nor were any terms hidden on the back of the form or in yet smaller print. Moreover, although the average person might not recognize the quality of the treatment from its description, if anyone could assess the quality of the described treatment or could ask intelligent questions about it, a professor of engineering like Bill probably could. Finally, Jake's sales puffing was transparently a form of salesmanship that should not have influenced Bill, and—although Jake visited Bill at home and rushed him somewhat—Bill had complete freedom to refuse Jake's terms and compare them with terms of other companies.

Substantive: Although BB's price was higher than those of other companies, and though the treatment described in the contract was at the lower end of the quality scale, the treatment could be sufficiently effective that it might indeed pay for itself with energy savings over the 7-8 year life of the treatment. The lack of an express warranty and the requirement of payment in advance are terms that favor BB's interests and not Bill's; however, they are not so unusual as to clearly justify the label of "oppressive." True, taken as a whole, the contract is lopsided in BB's favor, but its lopsided nature is apparent mostly in comparison with terms offered by other companies; the very fact that Bill had many options available to him undermines his argument for unconscionability.

Conclusion?

APPENDIX C

Sample Answers to Essay Exam Exercises in Chapter 11

I. FACT-BASED ESSAY QUESTION WITH A CERTAIN ANSWER

D. Exercise—UCC § 2-207

Acceptance

In contrast to the common law mirror-image rule, UCC § 2-207(1) recognizes a response to an offer as an acceptance, even if it contains additional or different terms, if the response is a definite and "seasonable" expression of acceptance and if it does not expressly condition acceptance on the offeror's agreement to the additional or different terms. A response is seasonable if sent within a time agreed or within a reasonable time (UCC § 1-204).

The question assumes that Buyer's purchase form is an offer. In the absence of Buyer's stating a time for acceptance, Seller's response time was clearly "seasonable," because Seller mailed it the same day as received, well within a reasonable time in a transaction calling for delivery within a month. Moreover, Seller definitely expressed acceptance with the handwritten message: "Your attached order is accepted. Expect delivery within two weeks." Because Buyer's order was attached to Seller's response, the response refers unequivocally to the order. Moreover, the statement about delivery within two weeks is entirely consistent with a commitment by Seller to accept an offer that calls for delivery within a month.

Seller's acknowledgment form contained a term not found in Buyer's offer: a mandatory arbitration term. However, Seller did not condition its acceptance of Buyer's offer on Buyer's assent to Seller's additional printed term. Consequently, under the liberal terms of section 2-207(1), Seller's response is an acceptance despite its inclusion of an additional term. At this point, the acceptance is on the terms of Buyer's offer.

Terms of the Contract: Modification?

Section 2-207(2) states that the additional terms in the acceptance are "construed as proposals for addition to the contract." In other words, under the UCC, Seller's additional terms in the acknowledgment form implicitly state an offer to modify the contract that was just formed on Buyer's terms. Moreover, between merchants, this proposal to modify will automatically be viewed as accepted—even in the face of Buyer's silence—unless Buyer's offer precludes such additions, unless the additions would materially alter the terms of the original offer, or unless Buyer has already objected to such additions or does so within a reasonable time after receiving the acknowledgment form.

The mandatory arbitration clause appears to be an additional term, because the topic of dispute resolution was not addressed in Buyer's offer. Thus, it is a proposal to modify the contract that was formed on Buyer's offer. Because the question states that both parties are merchants, the terms will automatically be added to the contract unless at least one of the three exceptions of section 2-207(2) applies.

The first exception does not apply because Buyer's offer did not preclude addition to the contract. The second exception might exclude the proposed addition on the ground of material alteration. However, uncertainty in the definition and application of that test precludes the second exception as a basis for a clear answer.

The third exception, however, does clearly apply. Buyer's statement that "[w]e object to private mandatory arbitration" was sent by e-mail immediately upon receipt of the additional terms. The proposed addition to the contract would thus be excluded by objection under the third exception to subsection 2.

Conclusion

Under UCC § 2-207(1), the parties reached agreement through their forms on the terms of Buyer's offer, and that contract does not require mandatory arbitration because the proposed addition to the contract was excluded under section 2-207(2) by Buyer's objections to them.

II. ESSAY QUESTIONS WITHOUT SUBSTANTIAL FACT ANALYSIS

B. Exercise—International Sale of Goods

Our client, the seller, would prefer to quietly allow the CISG to apply to this international transaction, rather than opt out of it and negotiate choice of the UCC.

If the UCC applied, section 2-601 would permit the buyer to reject the whole delivery for even a minor breach, because it permits the buyer to reject the entire shipment if the goods fail in any respect to conform to the contract. On rightfully rejecting the goods under section 2-601, the buyer could then cancel the contract under section 2-711.

In contrast, under articles 46 and 49 of the CISG, a buyer can reject goods and then can either demand a new delivery or cancel the contract only if nonconformity in the delivery amounts to a fundamental breach. Under article 25, a seller's breach is fundamental only if it substantially deprives the buyer of his contractual expectations.

Therefore, we should let the CISG apply. Our client will do its best to send 100% conforming goods. However, if the delivery includes some minor, insubstantial non-conformity, the buyer cannot reject the goods or cancel the contract, but can simply ask for a reduction in price.

Explanation of True–False and Multiple-Choice Exercises in Chapter 12

II. TRUE–FALSE QUESTIONS

C. True–False Questions with Fact Patterns

6. Exercise—Five True–False Questions Relating to Common Facts

1. *False.* The lower courts in a state cannot ignore even an outdated precedent of the highest court in the state, if the highest court has not overruled the precedent.

2. *True.* Precedent from Arizona is not binding on any court in another state.

3. *True. Smith v. Jones* is already exceptional, as the only case in the jurisdiction that awards punitive damages for breach of contract, and a surrogacy contract is sufficiently different in nature than a marriage contract to justify distinguishing the two.

4. *False.* Without the assistance of the legislature, the state's highest court can overrule its own precedent if it has good reason to do so, such as changes in society that make the precedent obsolete or outdated.

5. *True.* As the primary policy-making body in a state, the legislature can enact a statute that modifies or replaces contrary common law in the state.

V. EXERCISES: MULTIPLE CHOICE

A. Theories of Contract Liability

1. The following explanation of this question reflects principles stated in the *Restatement (Second) of Contracts* §§ 71, 77, 79 (1981). The correct answer is **A**.

A. Bob and Larry have exchanged promises with reciprocal inducement, and this statement excludes the possibility that they intended only social consequences to their statements.

B. So long as each person is promising to forbear from engaging in a legal activity, they are promising a valid performance, and it is unnecessary to show that they will suffer some sort of loss or other detriment in doing so.

C. So long as each person seeks the other's promise (is induced by it), it is unnecessary to show that he will derive some tangible benefit from the promised performance.

D. It's precisely because they have a legal right to drink and smoke that their mutual promises to abstain provide consideration.

E. Each promise states a commitment, so neither is illusory.

2. Choosing the illusory promise. The correct answer is **D**.

A. This may be a conditional gratuitous promise, and therefore not enforceable for lack of consideration; however, it is not illusory in the sense of explicitly leaving discretion whether to perform.

B. Once again, this promise may be gratuitous and therefore lack consideration, but it is not illusory; the only limit to its terms is a time limit outside the speaker's control.

C. UCC § 2-306 would make this non-illusory by implying an obligation to sell at least that output that would occur in good-faith operation of the plant, subject to economic conditions outside the speaker's control.

D. This is the illusory promise, because it permits the speaker to provide no consulting services at his or her own whim or unfettered discretion.

E. This sounds like a gratuitous promise, but it commits the promisor to perform for a time period that is not limited by the promisor's whim, so the promise is non-illusory.

3. This question asks whether an employer's promise to give a car to her retiring butler provides a basis for a remedy on any theory. The correct answer is **E**.

A. Promoting a theory of bargained-for exchange is wrong because it assumes that the employer promised to give the car in exchange for the former butler's promise to pick out the car and drive it away. However, without special facts, the butler's act of picking out the car is simply a means of his collecting the gift and not the employer's inducement for making the promise. In fact, she explains later that her only inducement in making the promise was to impress her friends.

B. Promoting a theory of contract based on moral obligation stemming from past services is weak because it fails to recognize that the employer paid the former butler a salary for the past services and thus owes no moral obligation, even if that were an accepted basis for enforcement. Even a court that would stretch the consideration doctrine to incorporate moral obligation likely would require much more compelling facts, such as a great injury to the butler and great, uncompensated benefit to the employer.

C. Promoting a theory of promissory estoppel is wrong because the butler did not rely on the promise before learning that it would not be performed.

D. Promoting a theory of quasi-contract is wrong because the butler provided the benefits of his 20 years of service in exchange for room, board, and a salary. He had no reasonable expectation of compensation beyond that for which he bargained.

E. Concluding that the retiring butler has no legal claim on the theories we have studied is correct. The employer may be lacking in moral character, but contract law does not purport to regulate every breach of social standards of ethics or morality.

B. Five Civil Procedure Questions Based on Extensive Common Facts

Explanations have been provided by Professor Bob Dauber. References are to the Rules of Federal Civil Procedure.

1. The correct answer is **C**.

A. Incorrect because the Complaint was personally served, so the additional time to answer when defendant returns a waiver of service does not apply.

B. Incorrect because default must be entered by the clerk under Rule 55(a) before a plaintiff may apply for a default judgment.

C. Correct.

D. Incorrect because the rules impose no such restriction on an application for default judgment.

E. Incorrect; this is the time for exchanging initial disclosures under Rule 26(a).

2. The correct answer is **D**, which posits that A-C are correct.

A. Correct under Rules 12(g) and (h).

B. Correct; a defendant has 14 days to respond to the Complaint after a motion to dismiss is denied under Rule 12(b).

C. Correct; the timing under Rule 26(a) runs from the date of defendant's first appearance, which, in this case, is the date on which the motion to dismiss was filed.

D. Correct, because it chooses all of the above.

E. Incorrect, because it chose A and B only.

3. The correct answer is **B**.

A. Incorrect, because Rule 26(a) requires each party to voluntarily disclose documents they may use as exhibits at trial; failure to disclose could preclude defendant from using the documents.

B. Correct. See A above.

C. Incorrect, because the documents could not have been produced "in anticipation of litigation" if they existed before Fertilife hired Draper.

D. This strategy is far too risky, because Fertilife would be unable to use the exhibits if Algor's witnesses did not make a statement that could be directly impeached by the documents.

E. Incorrect, because only B is correct.

4. The correct answer is **C**.

A. Incorrect, because any person with relevant information may be deposed under Rule 30.

B. Incorrect. Under Rule 26(d), no discovery may be initiated until the parties have conferred under Rule 26(f), which takes place after the parties have exchanged disclosures.

C. Correct. See B above.

D. Incorrect; interrogatories may not be served on non-parties.

E. Incorrect, because B and D are incorrect.

5. The answer is **D** because it is the only *incorrect* response.

A. Correct. Only documents that a party expects to use to support its claim or defense need be disclosed under Rule 26(a).

B. Correct. Rule 26.1(a)(9) requires a party to voluntarily disclose documents relevant to the subject matter of the litigation.

C. Correct. While Rule 11 sanctions will not be imposed if the attorney had a good faith basis to believe the position taken was supported by the facts and law, based on a reasonable investigation, at the time the document was signed, sanctions may be imposed for later advocating a position once the lawyer knows it is not supported by the law.

D. Incorrect, because the e-mail was not created in anticipation of litigation.

E. Correct, under Rule 34.